T0208597

Finding Immortality

The Making of One American Family

HERBERT HADAD

iUniverse, Inc.
New York Bloomington

Finding Immortality
The Making of One American Family

Copyright © 2009 Herbert Hadad

iUniverse books may be ordered through booksellers or by contacting:

iUniverse
1663 Liberty Drive
Bloomington, IN 47403
www.iuniverse.com
1-800-Authors (1-800-288-4677)

ISBN: 978-1-4401-8931-9 (pbk)
ISBN: 978-1-4401-8933-3 (cloth)
ISBN: 978-1-4401-8932-6 (ebk)

Printed in the United States of America

iUniverse rev. date: 11/16/2009

This compelling memoir by an award-winning writer and teacher illuminates the joys and sorrows of his young family's life with humor and insight and, especially, uncompromising honesty.

Praise from Pulitzer Prize–winning author Lawrence Wright: "These gritty and flavorful essays address the emotional costs of virtue, faith, and true love."

In this lyrical and poignant book, *Finding Immortality: The Making of One American Family*, award-winning writer Herbert Hadad records the joys and sorrows of parenthood and, in so doing, opens a wide window into family life that is intimate and unmistakably American. The masterful prose of *Finding Immortality* conveys the true tale of one family confronting and triumphing over real issues, from infidelity and drink to mortality and racism. These universal themes provide a treasury of lessons for parents and all other admirers of fine writing to learn and enjoy. Here is what some readers have had to say about *Finding Immortality*:

"These gritty and flavorful essays address the emotional costs of virtue, faith, and true love."
—Lawrence Wright, winner of the Pulitzer Prize in nonfiction for *The Looming Tower* and staff writer for *The New Yorker*

"An elegant writer and story teller, Hadad spins tales as compelling as O'Henry's. These are vivid, often roguish, portraits of the angst and pleasures of contemporary existence."
—Selwyn Raab, author and retired *New York Times* reporter

"Kid boxer and life-long journalist Herb Hadad has been around. He's seen a lot. Part Jew, part Arab, and all American, he loves his children, his wife, and his world. These stories will clear the mind and warm the heart."
—Benjamin H. Cheever, novelist and journalist

"As strong as the bonds are among Herbert Hadad's family members in these pellucid domestic narratives, he makes clear that as a father he has as many faults as the next guy. These are not stories about suburban Care Bears. Yet the episodes flow so smoothly that you imagine it must be easy to do this kind of writing. It isn't."
—Stephen S. Pickering, retired *New York Times* staff editor

"Herb Hadad distills with a great eye and a great ear what we care about and presents it brilliantly, with wit and understanding."

—Dr. Myles Striar, professor of education emeritus, Boston University, writer, and translator

"Hadad doesn't blink, he doesn't flinch. He looks straight at his subjects, sometimes in sorrow but mostly in joy, and tells the stories that dwell in most of us. *Finding Immortality* is a wonderful read."
—the late Dennis Duggan, columnist, *Newsday*

"His essays are personal and quirky, with an angle, a larger theme, that makes them stick and gives them an edge. The big test: as a reader it is hard not to care about Herbert Hadad and his family. I think of E.B. White here, how he could make his geese, his dachshund Fred, his neighbor with the plow, himself with doldrums, all off-center and yet universal, something we understood. He made his little world feel connected to ours, us to him. That's the gift. I think Herbert does that."
—Geraldine Van Dusen, editor and freelance journalist

Herbert Hadad is an award-winning writer and former contributing reporter and essayist for *The New York Times*. He currently serves as a press officer for the U.S. Department of Justice and teaches writing for the Hudson Valley Writers' Center. He has lectured at prominent universities and appeared at Symphony Space, New York's renowned performance center. His work has appeared in nationally recognized magazines and anthologies. He and his wife live in Pocantico Hills, New York, and have three children.

Photo of the author by Charles Aram Hadad
Cover photo by Edward Salim Hadad, taken in Pocantico Hills, New York

To my parents

Who gave me the dream

To Evelyn

Who made it come true

Contents

Introduction

"Marriage is the only adventure open to the cowardly." That expression has tickled me ever since I became a family man. It sounds so right, but it is so wrong. I looked it up and it belongs to Voltaire. That says a lot. It says that Voltaire, a philosophical giant of the Enlightenment, didn't know legumes about married life. It says he never found the right Mrs. Voltaire.

I had my share of adventures before marriage. As a small boy, I defeated an entire gang of neighborhood toughs merely by putting a yarmulke on my head. "Take it off and fight fair!" they yelled. They would have beaten me up for being different from them, but the little black cap stopped them cold.

A Jew with an Arabic name, an Arab with a Jewish religion learns to be a fighter. I became a boxer. When the promoter decided an Arab would draw more customers, I was billed by my real name. When the promoter wanted a Jewish warrior, or a Jewish victim, to attract the fight fans, I became Abe Finkel, taking the name of the local druggist. I even wore blue-and-white satin trunks. I got blood on them.

I ran races, fifty- and one-hundred-yard dashes. Many times, my chest split the twine at the finish line. My name was in the papers. I was a newspaper reporter. I saw a fat man who had been shot in the stomach die on the operating table just as the police detective—I had slipped by the hospital guards and nurses by posing as his partner—said, "Who did this to you?"

I met politicians, aristocrats, millionaires, and entertainers when their guards were down. I was hired to give advice to a man who ran for President of the United States. I was asked by two women to sleep with them at the same time. I climbed a mountain with a friend; we toasted our arrival at the top with daiquiris in crystal glasses.

But even as these various events unfolded, I longed to be a husband and a father. I sensed deeply that the greatest adventures awaited in making a family and making a home. Answering this longing wouldn't be as easy as it appeared to be.

On one first date, I blurted out my fondest hope, my deepest dream. "I want to be a family man. I want to have thirteen children and a big house, with the kids coming and going and bringing tales of excitement, and seeking solutions to their problems and feeling that our home is the one place in the whole world where they can always come and feel loved and protected."

That became our last date as well.

As I arrived in my late twenties and early thirties, I became an uncle, at times feeling the little nephews were virtually my own infants. The thought that they were someone else's could, in weak moments, make me cry. The only compromise I made with my dream was numerical.

"I want to be a family man," I said late one night to a sensual, high-spirited, nurse outside her residence. "I want to have eight children." Her goals were slightly more short-term. She broke apart a fresh six-pack. "Let's have another beer and wait for the sunrise," she replied.

Many years and experiences later, I met Evelyn. After a captivating courtship, she agreed to marry me. She shared my feelings about family life. By then I had reduced the number of hoped-for children to five. Evelyn talked about three. She and I trained to be together for the first birth. We made giddy jokes about the breathing techniques and counting and coaching. But I was on a slow train home when Evelyn gave us a son we called Edward Salim, after her late father and my father's long-gone brother, who had remained in the Middle East.

For days afterward, well-wishers wanted to know why I was limping. The reason was my excessive celebration of fatherhood. I had seen Evelyn as a mother for the first time and my new son. I had kissed them, left the hospital, and broken into a run, running uphill all the way to our street two miles away. And then, instead of returning to our empty house, I had continued to run, through the woods until it was dark, until I was in a state of exhausted bliss.

Evelyn would give us two more children, Charles Aram, named for my father's closest brother and for the ancient name of Syria, and Sara Jameela, after his sister, dead for half a century, alive enough in memory to make my father cry. The Jameela was my idea, Arabic for beautiful. Like all delighted, self-involved parents, we took pictures of Edward, Charles, and Sara, but hundreds or thousands of snapshots weren't enough.

I also wanted to be a writer. I had no desire now to join revolutions or chase bulls or go on safaris, for I was finding that stoking the home fires was the great adventure I thought it could be. I experienced in our household enough moments of joy or tears to occupy a lifetime.

And I began to see stories in these daily events. I decided that writing was how I would express and record our early lives together— through stories that might even last beyond a lifetime and impart a kind of immortality. These are those stories. Many have enjoyed earlier publication in magazines and newspapers. They begin with the children barely out of infancy and end with the oldest of them at the onset of biblical manhood, going on twelve. (There are two exceptions. "On Defining Family" is a personal account of the events of September 11, 2001, and its aftermath. "Journey through the Land of the Gaels" describes the essential role of the Irish in my life.) Of course my family, like all families, did not spring whole from the hopes and passions of two people. It would indeed be a conceit, an oversight, not to include in-laws, grandparents, even older ancestors, so they, too, make appearances.

One last thought: Nothing would give me greater delight than for you to read these stories, recognize the characters that inhabit them and, except for the names and places, realize these are your stories as well.

Missing Nelson

I never met the man in my life. My feeling about all his money and power was inarticulate awe. I wondered often what he was like as a small boy, what he was told about who we are and why we're here. I wondered whether what he was told was different from what I now tell my own boys. I felt sorry for him twice: when he was snookered out of the Republican nomination for president and when he made a lewd gesture at a heckler. I coveted his vast property at Pocantico Hills, New York—so close to my modest house—and still do. I am not certain how I feel about the way he died, though I am inclined to believe the most scandalous version. I do know that I miss Nelson Rockefeller.

That must sound strange. Out of the blue one day, I told my wife I was going to write a story and the title was going to be, "My First Season Without Nelson." Evelyn, who is young and lovely and amiable, thought that was funny. I felt curiously hurt. The notion of that title had glided into my head one day about six months after Nelson's death, as I jogged around the Tarrytown Lakes at the edge of the Rockefeller property, near where Lake Road rises to the Pocantico Hills itself and the deer come down in the early morning and again before sunset to graze.

Evelyn was certainly right. The idea that I experienced longing for Nelson Rockefeller was silly and odd. But it stayed with me and became particularly poignant when I ran up Bedford Road, which winds through part of the estate. I imagined where Rockefeller might have enjoyed a pause beside the small frog pond, ordered the planting of a tree, or gazed over his domain and, perhaps, drew in big, luxurious breaths of contentment.

Then what was different for me now? The estate remained as beautiful as ever. I was free to roam over its bridal paths, along pastures, across meadows, with no more problem than an occasional suspicious or sullen look from a workman.

When they were old enough to take long walks, I introduced my two sons to the estate. We climbed a hill east from Bedford Road, just before it rises and then dips steeply to reach an intersecting highway. Like their father, the boys quickly came to covet the land. I called the hill Edward and Charles Mountain once, and that's the name the hill became. At the crest of Edward and Charles Mountain, under a procession of gnarled apples trees, we could turn and face the west to enjoy a panorama of meadows and woods and, beyond them, the cliffs across the Hudson River and beyond them the hills and valleys of the next county.

My boys and I could spot horseback riders a mile or more away. One day, after instructing my two-and-a-half-year-old son on identifying hoof prints on a bridal path, using a small limb from an apple tree as a pointer, we arrived at a second path, and I took the moment to reinforce the lesson. Tracing the shape with the pointer, I asked, "What's that, Charles?" He put his hands on his knees, crouched down to inspect the spot and said, "That's mud." He filled me with humbling laughter.

Under the stone bridge at the foot of Edward and Charles Mountain, all three of us developed a kinship with echoes. When we returned home from these expeditions, the boys always brought mementos. They were only dried dead branches, but we had done something special and that required special equipment. They called the mementos their walking sticks.

The winter before my longing arose I had visited the Rockefeller estate as a newspaper reporter, entering the grounds behind the village green between high stone gate posts and arriving at a simple house-like building of cut stone that served as an estate office. That day the building became the headquarters for the reporters and photographers covering Nelson's funeral.

Family aides, burying their careers as well as their master, provided details of the event, thoughtfully and carefully, loyal to the end. Nelson's cremated remains were placed in the ground of a family plot. During the graveside service, his teenage son read a poem he had composed, expressing longing for his dad.

The next time I entered the stone building, it was to scoop most of the domestic and international press gathered at a court house in White Plains, New York, to await details of Nelson Rockefeller's will. Another reporter and I felt correctly that aides at Pocantico Hills might be more forthcoming than the polite but obviously uncooperative Wall Street lawyer handling the probate in White Plains.

Having been a reporter for a long time, I had developed a chronic disdain for politicians, maybe more than they deserved. Nelson was a politician, but when he had been alive he could come nowhere near my feelings for the only politician I had once openly missed, John F. Kennedy.

No, it had to be something else. I sensed it had to be connected to the proximity of his estate and my home—chosen by Evelyn and me shortly after our marriage, the place to which we brought our two infant sons and, later, our new daughter. The unearned pride of living so close to Pocantico Hills—where royalty and heads of state would flock, where momentous decisions were pondered, ribaldry indulged, grief contained—had to have something to do with it.

Being able to dart out of my front door and trace virtually the entire Rockefeller estate on foot and then run home again—that had to have something to do with it. And being there to bury Nelson, then derive notoriety from digging into his affairs—that had to figure in it, too.

But it took me a very long time to realize that when he was put in the ground, as his two young sons in their black suits stared, that was the core of our bond. I missed Nelson. I longed for him. I wished he continued to roam his great estate, for his mortality seeped into my brain and then lodged in my heart. I wanted to feel I could stay on Edward and Charles Mountain with my boys forever. Nelson taught me I could not.

Daughters

Before dawn this day, my little daughter fusses and tumbles over the terrain of bumpy comforters and billowed pillows to plant a gentle, soundless kiss on the cheek.

She joins me in the bathroom, making sympathetic small talk when I cut myself shaving, then returns to the bedroom to help me select a tie. "That's pretty" is the assessment that clinches the choice, especially on mornings when for an inexplicable but vaguely disturbing reason I might try on five and find them all ludicrous.

In the midst of my rush to be on time, she hugs my leg as the fireman might embrace the fire pole, then she lets go and challenges me to catch her and tickle her. She takes in good humor that she cannot borrow my Groucho glasses at the moment, and I think that Sara Jameela, not yet three years old, is the best daughter a man could hope for.

The railroad strike is still on this day, and at the station a crowd waits, with tolerance but not patience, for the bus to take commuters from the suburbs to the subways and another ride to the city. A woman between twenty and thirty years old—fair and plump, well-dressed, and wearing glasses—is among the first to board. She takes one of the very front seats that, on buses designed for schoolchildren, affords the adult passenger a little more precious space. I board a few persons later and begin to sit down next to her.

"Oh, no, you don't!" she yells. I express my surprise by saying something to the effect of, "Come now, I'd like that seat."

She turns savage. She presses both her hands against my rib cage and hurls me across the aisle. Her voice is shrill, profane, and sacred at the same time as she screams: "I am saving this seat for my mo-ther!" A glum, silent, middle-aged woman takes the seat.

At the office, the photo in a weekly newspaper ambushes the reader. It is of a girl, age seven, looking shy and pretty. The coarseness of the newsprint does not allow you to really determine what you think you see—that her lashes are missing and her hair is a wig. The ten paragraphs next to the picture hit like hammer blows.

She suddenly asks one morning, goes the story, to be wheeled around her house. "She was going from room to room saying good-bye to things," her father related. "She said good-bye to her little brother and to the cats, and then turned to us and said, 'Oh, my little heart is breaking, but I must leave you now.'" On the way to the doctor she strains to look through the rear window of the car for a last look at her home. She is dead of cancer the next day.

On a Manhattan street at lunchtime a co-worker and I pass a girl who appears fourteen or fifteen years old leaning against the entrance of a dilapidated rooming house. She is homely and overweight, and her skin is going to gray. She is wearing white cowgirl boots and a blue polyester sweater-and-skirt outfit that reveals much of her legs. She casts passersby a dull look, senses no interest, then looks beyond them to nowhere in particular.

My companion comments with casual flippancy that he sure hopes she is there when we walk by thirty minutes later. "I hope not," I say. "Don't forget that she's somebody's daughter." He looks ashamed for a moment, and I tell him to take it easy on himself. On the way back, she is gone. We are glad, frankly, not to have to see her.

This night when I arrive home Sara Jameela is waiting at the door that leads to the garage. She races to me and I catch her and raise her up in one swooping motion until we are hugging each other tightly.

"My Daddy," she says, full of pride and possession.

I hate to let her go. I think of her, and I think of the little girl in the newspaper, and the teenager in boots, and the young woman on the bus. Spare my girl, I say to myself, and I hug her three times more.

Mysticism

It's a little too early to tell if my son Charles is a full-fledged mystic. But by age three he already had an uncanny ability to weave delicate connections and to shape bold, pure insights.

This is not the mere babbling of a proud papa. Charles has a brother, a year older, and a sister, two years younger, and both of them are unusually bright and charming—a statement I would make under oath but make here anyhow to ensure domestic tranquility and avert an uproar from the grandparents. But it has been Charles's findings that have been particularly startling and enriching. And he is now only six.

Charles was painfully stung by a bee that had flown into the family station wagon while it was parked at a shopping center. When the family returned and got in, Charles got it. He cried at the hurt, felt soothed by the treatment and the sympathy, and talked about the bee for a few days. But all the time he was privately sifting the details of the event so that he could arrive at an explanation satisfactory to his own understanding of the world around him.

"Why do jellyfish sting?" is how he began his conversation with me when he had done all the thinking he needed.

"Because they think you're going to hurt them, and that is nature's way of protecting them, giving them a weapon in case they need it," I told him.

The subject derived from a family stay on the North Fork of Long Island, New York, a year earlier, a glorious time during which the children were introduced to some of the wonders of the sea, including jellyfish. Neither Charles nor his brother and sister were stung, despite their occasional animosity toward the jellyfish.

"Then why do bees sting?" Charles asked.

"Same reason," I said. "When they see a person swinging at them, they think they're being attacked, so they sting."

"But I didn't swing, I was just sitting there, and he stung me on the arm."

"I know, Charles, and I'm sorry it happened, but the bee thought you might hurt him."

Charles was not about to purchase what I considered a solid and logical explanation. He was merely testing my hypothesis against his own.

"The bee stung me," he concluded without a trace of doubt in his voice, "because he thought I was a flower."

Charles happens to be a handsome tyke whose skin, hair, and disposition are as smooth as honey. When I thought about it, I couldn't begin to challenge the beauty of his perception of the bee. I first became aware of Charles's skill at insight during our seaside vacation. By age three Charles, like most every other youngster in America, had had his share of hamburgers as well as his share of falls, cuts, and scrapes. Charles, however, saw a connection. One morning, nowhere near a hamburger or an accident, he announced, "I like ketchup, but I don't like blood."

All the children love a turn with the garden hose, watering the flowers and vegetables, and—they always say it's inadvertent—each other. After one watering session, Charles watched with quiet attention as I grabbed the hose in a kind of afterthought and starting washing old cobwebs and other leavings of nature off the walls and shutters of our home.

"That won't make the house grow," he declared almost immediately, as though he wanted to spare me disappointment later in the season.

Charles also seems to have a well-developed sense of adult decorum. As he, his brother, and I passed a pharmacy, Edward poked Charles in the side and urged him to study the life-size poster of a bronzed woman in a string bikini promoting sun tan lotion.

Trying to defuse the sexual impact of the display with nonchalance, I said, "What's the big deal, guys? Just a woman wearing a bathing suit."

"But not all of it, Daddy," said Charles.

Sometimes existing vocabulary proved inadequate, such as one day when we were meandering over a beach. Charles had run ahead, and he suddenly stopped in a state of agitated excitement. He reached down into the sand and raised up an iridescent conch shell, with its complex structure of tubes and curves and cubbyholes.

"Subiyasa!" he shouted back to us, "subiyasa!"

Not knowing what he had found but stirred by its beauty and his delight in finding it, Charles had invented the word. A year later we moved into a house large enough for our growing family on a woods-laden sweep of land in a community we had long-admired but had never expected to call our own. We call our place "Subiyasa."

First Day

Little boys and girls are supposed to cry and rush back to the comfort of their parents' knees when the bus pulls up for that momentous first day of school. It didn't work out that way at our house. First of all, there was confusion over the bus schedule, and my wife drove Edward Salim to school. Second, someone else did the crying.

I was nervous from the second I rolled out of bed. "Where is Edward? Still asleep? My goodness, he has to be up and out and alert as he can be in just over an hour."

Edward's brother and sister, who were not yet about to enter the crucible of education, were up early, chatting, catching a few cartoons on the tube, helping me select a tie, dabbling at their breakfasts.

Edward was playing it cool. When he did arrive downstairs, I must admit I was all over him, clucking, explaining, beseeching, instructing. To Edward, I must have seemed like a cross between a stage mother and a frantic prizefight handler working his corner between rounds. Bobbing and weaving in and out of my broadcast area, the boy took it all in like a pro, calmly nodding at every tense and meaningful commandment I was sending forth.

When he turned his head to watch Sylvester the Cat for a moment, I reacted with a gruesome lecture on how television pickles the brain and leaves the child wobbling in the starting blocks of life. Edward graciously turned away from the television set. I admired his calmness. He reminded me now of a great bullfighter about to enter the arena, or a seasoned track star wiggling away the last traces of tension before the big event.

In reality, I was probably imbuing him with all these heroic traits, and all he was doing was behaving like a sweet little boy who's just awakened and is going to school today rather than swim or play with his brother and sister on the front lawn or cut out a feathered headdress.

Maybe I was coming on too strong. His mother and I discussed what Edward was going to wear to school. That subject seemed less inflammatory. Edward has very particular taste, so naturally he participated. We had long ago banned the notion of jeans. Denim narcissism and corridors of accomplishment were just not compatible, we said. No argument. The blue trousers and brown leather shoes were accepted all around quickly. Discussion turned to the color and type of shirt, and whether a vest was needed on this cool morning, and how the vest would affect the rest of the ensemble.

All these colossal decisions were being made, mind you, while I also shaved and dressed and collected papers for my satchel for the trip to the big city, where I would continue to make other big decisions for eight or more hours, not including lunchtime.

When I had done all I could, I went quietly. Was Edward secretly glad it was time for me to dash to the train? No, he gave me an extra good-bye, lingering on the word "Dad-dee" in a way that always breaks my heart a little.

Five minutes later I drove by the schoolhouse where Edward, God willing, would study for the next nine years. I turned my head toward it for a moment. "Good luck, Edward," I said. I was surprised when I started to cry. "Good luck, my darling."

Declarations of Independence

Of course, the children think I'm nuts, but I line them up anyhow and deliver my speech: "Don't call. Never mind the dinner invitations. I don't feel like going fishing. I know you want to be nice, but your mother and I have too much to do. You can do us a favor and let us give you a call. We're too busy for anything right now."

They peer at each other and smile those magical smiles that say our daddy is a loon, but we love the loon so let's stand here until he's finished.

Our children are five, four, and two years old. I miss them if I leave the house before they're awake, yet I'm trying to establish between us an advance kind of independence. They seem to know that I'm speaking to them at more than one level, even if the message is confusing. I have to concede that it confuses me, at least a little, as well. Last year, I watched them from the screened porch of a beach house we had rented. They were frolicking in the sand and sea grass at the edge of a broad serene cove just as the morning sun stabbed through the haze.

"Look at them," I said to myself. "How beautiful they are. I don't think I'll be happier as long as I live."

I had fallen in love with a tableau. But when I realized the moment would be gone and irreplaceable, I soon became sad rather than happy. The insight did not break my melancholy habit. I fell in love with tableaux afterward, but having been burned by this form of parental madness once, I fell afterward not so deeply or hard.

One evening, the three of them trailed me down to the garden to help carry back what turned out to be pound after pound of overripe tomatoes. There was the tableau again. A crisp and fragrant time shortly before sunset, tanned faces and toes, pure joy over the task of transporting the fruit to the kitchen. I fell in love with them all over again.

But this time I was different. It was a happier love. I had learned there was no need to fret that the moment would soon be lost forever. In fact, it stayed rather comfortably in my mind and heart. Now I can summon it anytime I wish.

I sometimes think that their mother has been pegged as a loon, too, but she smiles when I deliver my orations to the troops. Maybe she is also loving them too much and feels a little distance is a good idea.

"Children, if I told you once I told you a hundred times. Don't call us unless you absolutely have to. We'll call you. We had you long enough. We love you like mad, but don't tie up the phone. Get the message? Good. Over and out."

They titter and nod and swap those tight-lipped grins, for to smile openly is somehow to laugh at Daddy, and Daddy is trying to make some sort of serious point here.

The whole matter was crystallized on a recent Sunday morning. I was taking the children to the store for the newspapers and their weekly rewards of gum and sports cards. "Take the slow route home," urged Evelyn, seeking a breather from all of us.

So I took them over to a porch sale advertised on a telephone pole, and at that house, for fifty cents, found the wisdom that expressed what I was trying to do all along. It was a small wall hanging showing a large gnarled tree and two birds soaring in the distance. Beneath the picture were the words: "There are only two lasting things/You can leave your children/One is roots/The other is wings."

Astonished by its simplicity and beauty, I rushed us home and immediately tacked up the picture on a bathroom wall, where I would see it the first thing each morning.

Still, a question remains, and it is not an easy one to answer. Who am I protecting with my declaration of independence? My beloved children, or myself?

When

One of my sons is already six, the other just became five. Their sister recently was three. They are wonderful company, full of humor and surprising insights. Their capacity to be impish or affectionate seems boundless. They are beautiful to see in motion and to watch in repose.

This evening, before dusk, they are out with me, working the land, cutting back thorny vines, weeding, feeding specimen bushes. I reward them with hugs. They fill me, at times, with a sadness I cannot comprehend.

My wife Evelyn and I attend a meeting at the school. The guest speaker is a child psychiatrist. Despite the endless ribbon of degrees and honors ascribed to him when he is introduced, the psychiatrist is informal and decidedly unpretentious. After a brief lecture on bringing up children, he asks for questions from the parents. The questions are immediate, difficult, profound. The doctor listens with concern, asks his own questions, and gives careful answers.

Children do argue; they will say white when you say black; they aspire to autonomy; the idea is to give in on some issues, he tells one parent.

There are many reasons why a child refuses to go to sleep, he tells another. Maybe he isn't tired. Maybe he is frightened because his bedroom is so far from the family downstairs.

Your girl, he tells one parent, shouldn't really be permitted to shut her door to visitors. You should encourage her to spend more time with friends and others who visit your house.

I admire the parents for their ability to ask questions that certainly trouble and probably embarrass them. A question comes to my mind and settles like an uncomfortable weight. I rehearse it but can't seem to raise my hand or stand to speak.

Someone else's daughter wants her own phone. The psychiatrist asks: Does she make a lot of calls? Well, then there must be another reason. Does her sister have her own phone? Are there things she does not want to talk about, things that she can discuss with friends but not with you? Try to see why the personal phone seems so important to her.

The applause is sincere and hearty when the session ends. The psychiatrist says he must dash to pack for a morning flight to his own daughter's college. Although he encouraged her to enroll at a university close to home, she had held out for one in the Midwest. It is a relevant anecdote, having to do with knowing when a parent has to let go and recognize a child's new passion for independence.

Evelyn and I discuss the meeting during the ride home. "What was the question you didn't want to ask?" she says.

"I wanted to know when you have to stop hugging them."

Returning to the Scene

When I was five years old and stood at our window looking into the bleak winter street, I would see the big old tree that had pushed away the sidewalk as if to establish itself forever.

On the days when my friends and I wandered down through Salem Willows to the shores, the tree would be the first image to seize my interest upon leaving the house and the last upon arriving home.

My family rented the first floor of the house, so my intimacy was with the lower section of the tree only; I had never seen it from the second floor or the attic.

Fifteen years later, my literature teacher, the dean of the college, said to write about what you know. So I wrote about Salem, Massachusetts, and the tree and how it became a sort of beacon for me as a small child. The dean was decidedly unimpressed. "Name the tree! What kind of tree?" he scrawled across the first page.

During a discussion of the story, I argued that a young boy would not necessarily know the species of even a tree that was an important fixture in his everyday life. "Nonsense," said the dean, and he gave me a C. I was angry with him.

In class a few weeks later, the dean said that since all the students were Americans, and Henry David Thoreau was an American, and we were studying him only a few miles from his onetime home, we would pronounce his name like an American—Henry David "Thorough."

I worked some nights as a copy boy on a newspaper. The morning after one of those nights, I nodded off while the dean was discussing his subject's love of nature and reliance on it. My indiscretion did not escape him.

"Mr. Hadad," he said, shaking me into consciousness, "did you study your Thorough last night?"

The dean wore a triumphant smirk on his little old face, while the class bubbled with snickers and giggles.

"Yes, Dean. Thoreauly," I said.

The class went wild. I was no longer angry with the dean, but the dean was with me. I got a C-minus for the course.

Fifteen years after that, I introduced the woman I would marry to my parents, who by then lived thirty-five miles from the old place in Salem. My mother was so taken with my choice that she slipped off her diamond ring and placed it on the younger woman's finger. This was done silently, in the back seat of the family car, as I drove my parents and girlfriend toward the shore for a Sunday outing.

I had noticed some activity in the rear-view mirror but knew what had happened only after a newly bejeweled hand was thrust forward for me to see.

"Congratulations, Mother," I said. "You and Evelyn just became engaged. I'm sure you'll be very happy." My father smiled his lovely white- and gold-toothed grin. We were all in a great mood.

"I've got an idea," I said. "Let's try and find the house in Salem where we lived when I was a little kid. Now that Evelyn is joining the family, it'll give her historical perspective. You know, Herb: the Early Years."

My mother said she had no great interest in the visit and predicted the search would fail. I wondered if returning to the place of her young motherhood might depress her. I also had learned as an adult that, although there had been affection between the landlord's family and my own, there had been many fights over the lack of heat.

"Ma, remember you went to the clerk of the court, and we had a hearing before a judge, and you put me on the stand, and the judge said, 'Don't be frightened, young man, just tell the truth,' and you served as your own lawyer, and we won our heat, not to mention the respect of the whole courthouse?"

In truth, I remembered nothing of the case. I recalled only the telling and retelling of the story over the years and that it became for our family a symbol of the beauty of justice and the benefits of what my mother called "speaking up."

"Yes, Herbie, of course I remember, but you don't know the half of it," my mother said in a lilting, dramatic voice, and we were on our way to Salem.

Finding the town was no problem, but once there I had no clues except that we had lived on Summit Avenue. Nonetheless, with hardly a wrong turn, we soon were cruising down my old street. After several minutes, I pulled up across from a neat, if weary-looking, white frame house with a big tree in front and said, "Okay, this is it."

Everyone else insisted on staying in the car until I rang the bell to see how well my memory had worked.

I went up to the door, and in a few moments there appeared a small, wiry man, of about eighty years old, with a twisted, acrid-smoking stogie in his mouth. He seemed to decide who I was and cried out in a sound that expressed, in one long syllable, both joy and grief. He tugged the stogie out of his mouth, stepped down, and kissed me strenuously on the lips.

I pulled back, my mouth and chin covered with bitter saliva, and waved to the people in the car, shouting, "I found our home! I found our home!" while wiping away a muzzle of brown juices.

A big reunion followed. The old man's wife had died, but in the house were two daughters, a son, and many grandchildren. After sampling several homemade red wines, I did an imitation of how I must have walked across the very same living room as a tot, moving fast, listing, almost falling, regaining my balance, and continuing.

I went to the front window and looked out. This, too, was a reenactment, for I had studied over the years a fuzzy photograph, more in shades of gray than black and white, of a little boy standing in the same window.

And then I focused on my tree. It was even bigger with age, and I was grateful that my grown-up perception of it did nothing to diminish its size.

"It wasn't the house I found," I said later in the car. "It was that big old tree. And, you know what, I still don't know what kind it is."

"It's a white oak," Evelyn said, meaning to be helpful. "Even at this time of year, you can tell from the shape of the twigs and the few leaves that have managed to hold on."

I was struck by a strangely resentful feeling. I wondered for a moment if I was becoming frightened at the prospect of marriage. But, the feeling passed. I knew I loved her and was thrilled that she loved me. So I drove without speaking and began dreaming of the fine times ahead for my future wife and me, and of my mother's generosity and my father's smile. I would have to sort out in time why I felt so close to Salem that morning and so distant now.

Death

It was a melancholy time, in between the vital warmth of summer and the chilling tests of winter, when I ambled over our slender estate with my five-year-old son Charles Aram. My mood lost not a moment seizing upon the age comparison: the father already treading in his autumn, the son barely embarked upon his spring.

We found and disposed of a stiffened bird, a young blue jay. Charles wanted to save it for his brother and sister. A neighbor and a police officer came to the door asking if the calico cat found struck and dying in the road was ours. It wasn't. A few minutes later there was the report of a single, merciful shot.

The summer had taken a financial toll as well, with lightning destroying our water system and maybe our favorite tree (spring would give us the answer) and the refrigerator experiencing a terminal collapse. The repairman had struggled behind the machine for a while, regaining his footing to announce, "It's the compressor; it just went. It's like having a heart attack." We had the appliance store cart it away to be tumbled into an appliance graveyard somewhere, and a new one was plugged in.

A mysterious dread called AIDS had taken a good friend, swiftly and unexpectedly, a few months earlier, and I found myself spending a lot of time asking why. So this day Charles and I were out watching the season take its toll, and the feeling in the air was a bit morose.

"Dad, birds die, don't they?" Charles asked, in the cadence he normally uses to verify what he already knows.

"Yes, darling, they do."

"Why, Dad?"

"Well, sometimes bad weather can kill them, or they can't get enough to eat, or an animal catches them, or they just grow old and die."

He thought it over. "And, Dad, animals"—he got it right, though he still says "aminals" half the time—"can die, right?"

"Yes, Charles, and for the same kinds of reasons as birds."

"And, Dad, people die, too, don't they?"

The frigid day, with its suggestion of the end of things, and Charles's conversation, questioning the most profound in what is still the voice of a babe, hit home hard. I felt burdened by sadness and self-pity.

"Yes, my Charles, and people die."

"And you know what else, Dad?"

"What, dear?"

"Refrigerators can die, too."

A weight lifted and disappeared. I laughed, almost giddy. "Bless you, Charles. You're the greatest." He contemplated that superlative.

"So is Mommy and Edward and Sara," he reminded me, wisely.

Blame

I never call my daughter "Princess" for fear she will grow up to be one. This is much easier said than done, for she is four years old and I adore her. I want her to understand that beauty comes from within, that a person who depends on good looks alone courts disappointment.

Her name doesn't help. In an attempt to satisfy a mix of ethnic, traditional, and phonic sensibilities, we named her Sara Jameela. It sounded like a good idea at the time. Sara means "princess" in Hebrew; Jameela means "beautiful" in Arabic. The task now is to bring her up without letting her succumb to all the vanities of a Princess Beautiful.

I am forty years older than Sara Jameela. At times I feel that is cruel. I may hope to enjoy her growing-up and will be the recipient of her profuse affection, but then may shuffle off before she's ever in any real trouble. Merely imagining her bringing home some boy, who may or may not have taken liberties, turns me into a dervish of spewing anger.

Were she to come to me with a career problem, moral confusion, mental illness, a troubled marriage, a legal tangle, serious disease—I don't know. Maybe I could rise to the occasion, but just now I feel too much simple fatherly joy to think I could be of any practical use.

If Sara Jameela is not one of the most beautiful girls in the world, she must be a contender. She is certainly the embodiment of eons of beauty beyond what I ever expected to help produce, even with my lovely wife. In photographs she appears demure, shy, but her dad knows that's just one fraction of her charm. Even at four years old, she is too wise to let a camera catch her magic.

She is the youngest of our three children and the only girl. She is the darkest. In a society that fawns on lightness, I cherish the exception. Her hair is deep brown and wavy, and she has a woman's way of brushing it away from her eyes with the back of her hand. Her forehead is generous, indicating her formidable intelligence. Her eyebrows are twin promontories above her immense, chocolate-colored pools of eyes, eyes that forecast the weather of Sara Jameela's spirit faithfully. When she is about to show hurt or anger, one can almost see the storms break across her eyes. When she is especially happy, or preparing to play a prank, such as tapping me on the back and vanishing before I can spin around, a dancing light returns, like the sun dispelling the clouds. Her eyelashes are wide, long fans that, when she opens and closes her eyes, create the illusion of slow motion.

Her dad's nose, bestowed by the Semites, rearranged in a long-ago sandlot football game, is nowhere to be found on her face; hers suggests the careful placement of a gumdrop. Her lips are rather thin, the upper one puckishly curved, and her smiles, like her eyes, can convey all manner of intentions.

She has been the favorite of visitors, babysitters, and passers-by for some time, but now she is being tested by peers. Each weekday morning she boards a school bus and, it is reported to me, the boys on the bus say, "Here comes 'The Face.'" It sounds fresh, whether the motive is appreciation or otherwise. My momentary concern that the boys were trying to be derogatory was soon dismissed as implausible. She is four, and she is The Face.

All my concerns about raising a princess aside, I believe I am generous in my treatment of Sara Jameela. "There can't be a little girl finer than you," I'll say. I feel obliged to include "little" for fear she should conclude she is more special than my wife Evelyn.

For the last two years Sara Jameela and I have played a game and, though the outcome is totally predictable, I had never grown tired of it until recently. It goes like this: We are in a group of females, such as with her aunt and grandmother, and I may say: "There is certainly an abundance of beauty here. Sara Jameela, who do you think is the most beautiful of all?"

Aware of the tale of the wicked queen and the mirror on the wall, I have refrained from playing the game in the company of vain women. Sara Jameela pretends to assess each female face around her, and her eyes start to dance and her lips wryly part. Then she juts out a hand as if to point to the winner of the contest. But at the last moment she curls the hand back to herself, finishing the gesture with a bounce of her forefinger off her chest and a grin. If you press her for clarification, she jabs herself again, stating, "Me, me," and laughs. She senses her immodesty and laughs to soften it.

A female kitten ingratiated itself to our household. Sara Jameela named it Megan after a girlfriend. One day, playing the game, I asked if either of the Megans might be more beautiful. The arm went out, curled back, and showed the winner. I had thought she might graciously claim runner-up to the kitten.

A short time later, giving my wife a breather, the three children and I took a walk in the woods and up through a meadow. One of the boys spotted a group of six deer. As we appeared to them at the top of a rise they ran into a hollow, where they were invisible. When we appeared in the hollow, they ran a hundred yards to the edge of the woods.

It was a wonderful game of hide-and-seek, lasting almost ten minutes. When the deer were sufficiently alarmed to bolt into the thicket for good, we stood around describing the enchanting event that had just ended. We three males asked whether the deer weren't the most beautiful things Sara Jameela had ever seen. She dispensed with the suspense of the meandering arm and, her eyes not sparkling, she tapped her chest. Her response had been humorless. My concern started to grow.

We were driving in the car, just Sara Jameela and I, to the supermarket on a late Saturday afternoon. We stopped at an intersection to allow three high-school cheerleaders to cross. They were dressed in red and white sweaters and short white skirts and still carried their pompons. They were pretty and animated, and I was momentarily lost in the reverie of my high-school cheerleaders and my inarticulate passions and their impossible wonderfulness. Sara Jameela raised herself up to her full three feet of height to look out at what was so interesting. "They're pretty," she said, "but I'm prettier." For the first time, I felt a sharp jolt of annoyance. She continued, "I'm prettier than them and prettier than Megan."

Sara Jameela is in the habit of calling me "my special Daddy" and "the best Daddy in the whole wide world" but I was mad at her now. I asked, "Who is more beautiful, is it you, or is it me?"

If there was confusion in her tremendous eyes, it came and went before I spotted it. She reached out, only this time her hand did not circle back to her chest. Instead she reached for my hand, raised it to her face and kissed it. She was telling me that she was more beautiful than I but that she did not want to hurt my feelings.

I was astonished by her sensitivity and perhaps a little unnerved imagining exactly what she thought I looked like. She had me on the ropes, but I was not going to give up without trying to make my point.

We arrived at the supermarket parking lot, and she released my hand, confident that I had been soothed. I asked her another question that I felt might get through. I felt it might also confound her, but I hoped it did not sound hostile.

"Sara Jameela, what makes you think you're so beautiful?"

She looked straight into my eyes. I saw the dance rising in hers. She opened her thin and curvaceous mouth and said, "You."

Sweet and Sour

My son Edward never sleeps with me. He is seven years old and the oldest of our three children. When the others have had nightmares or heard strange noises or awakened in the middle of the night and don't know why, they hustle down the stairs, rap at our door, and slip into bed with my wife and me. Edward fights his own demons, returns to sleep, and does not appear downstairs until daybreak.

He and I had a fight recently. I feel foolish saying so, more foolish over explaining why. He took some of my Chinese take-out dinner after he had finished his own. I did not understand my anger, and before I knew it, I slapped his face. My hand only grazed his cheek, but it was bad enough. I remember him saying, "But, Dad, it was only a little piece." I felt terrible and afraid.

Saturday morning, Edward did not appear. I went up, and he heard me coming and feigned sleep. He lay on his stomach, his face hidden. I talked to his back, touched his side, coaxed him to turn toward me, and asked for a hug. He put his arms around me tentatively, and I squeezed him hard and asked him to come downstairs.

I had an errand to run and asked him to accompany me. Once we were in the car, I told him what was on my mind.

"Edward, I apologize. I'm sorry for how I behaved last night." He only listened. "I had a drink. I was tired. I think if I hadn't taken that drink, I wouldn't have acted so poorly. Anyhow, I'm sorry, and I hope you'll accept that."

He was not eager to accept the apology. I knew he was still hurt, but he said, "Okay, Dad." I wondered then whether I admired or resented his aloofness and independence. I thought, both.

I told Edward a story about a man and his father and drinking. It's a true story, and it's been in my head for twenty years. I wasn't sure why it occurred to me at this moment, but I began to tell it and watched my son through the rear-view mirror and felt love at his rapt look.

"This man I know and his father were separated when the man was a youngster, and for several years there was no contact of any kind. The man I know, who became a friend, liked to drink. Maybe he drank because he liked it, maybe because it made him forget for a little while things that hurt him, maybe because he had heard his own dad liked to drink so much.

"My friend's wife was so upset with his drinking, however, that she tried to get him to stop by saying he could not drink in her presence."

Edward asked, "Did he go to barrooms instead?"

"No, strangely enough, he didn't go to barrooms very often. He was a family man, and he liked being home at night, for he had two or three little girls. But he wanted to drink, too. So on many nights he'd go down to the cellar by himself and drink beer until he was tired and sleepy, and then he'd come up and go to bed."

"But did the man ever see his dad again?" Edward wanted to know.

"Here's what happened. My friend decided he had to see his father at least once more in his lifetime. So he started searching. Every year when it was vacation time, instead of going on vacation, he'd go looking for his father.

"This went on for several years, and one summer he heard his father was up in Canada. So he jumped in his car and drove all the way to this city in Canada, and when he got there he made some phone calls and all of sudden he was talking to his father. I don't know what the first words were, Edward, but they agreed to meet in a certain barroom.

"So my friend found the place and walked in and there was his dad, already sitting on a stool. They shook hands and each said something like 'It's good to see you.' They had two or three drinks. Then the dad stood up, asked how my friend's mother was, said good-bye and walked out."

"Didn't your friend chase his dad down the street?" asked Edward with cold fascination.

"No, he didn't do anything like that. He had set out to see his father one more time, and he'd accomplished that. He seemed to realize there was no good reason to chase after him. His father had agreed to meet for a few drinks, nothing more. My friend sat there thinking for a little while, went back to his car, and started the long trip home."

Not long after telling the story, I fought with Edward again. Curiously, it was over Chinese food; he'd eaten the meat and brushed the vegetables into the garbage. My mind raced back to the first incident. I'd had a drink this evening, too. I did not raise my hand, but I was annoyed.

I told him to go and live with his grandmother, whom he had just visited, or with a neighbor up the road, where I knew the pleasures accorded the children are scant.

Edward, the aloof and independent one, responded with cries of self-pity, which only irritated me further. I shouted how I had to run for trains and fight my way onto subways and meet tough deadlines, and I was a fool if I were going to continue to do so just to let him throw away good food.

I finished my dinner alone and miserable while my wife put the children to bed. Feeling suddenly exhausted, I went to bed myself, listened for a few minutes to the radio news, and nodded off. When I awoke some time later, something extraordinary had happened. Edward was curled up against me. He didn't move, but I felt great relief at his presence and a wave of gratitude.

Never become the man searching for his father, I asked of my son. Never become the father waiting in the barroom, I promised myself.

Natural Causes

As we passed the spot on the road where the car and deer had collided, I called out, "Twoooooo-Six, Twoooooo-Six." Of course, the animal did not materialize.

"Why must you call him that?" asked my wife.

"Because '$2,623.81' is too long. And '$200 Deductible' seems a silly name for a ten-point buck."

The lady—the beautiful, sensitive, affable lady—was not amused. Evelyn had been by herself, behind the wheel on a cold, clear night when, not more than two-hundred yards from our house, the buck sprang across the road and into the path of our new car, forcing it into a ditch. She appeared in our bedroom doorway several minutes later. I'd been reading and was still awake. She was unhurt but very shaken and, I soon learned, already brimming with sorrow.

"He was so big that even on his knees his head was above the window. He had those huge antlers, and those large eyes—soft, brown eyes. I got out to see if he was okay …"

"You what? You should have stayed in the car. He could have charged at you!"

"But he didn't. He struggled to his feet and trotted back across the road and into the woods."

"Well, you're all right, that's the only important thing."

But it wasn't really. I felt a tangle of emotions, including anger because the car was new, because it had become "Dad's car," and because it was now and forever damaged.

"You'd better have a look at it," Evelyn said. "I was able to pull out of the ditch and drive it the rest of the way home, but I think it's pretty serious."

I dressed and went out with a flashlight and found the bumper and grill wrecked, the hood sprung out of alignment, rumpled steel where the right headlamp had been. I turned on the ignition, and the car started up and sounded the same as it had before, but there was in the moment an almost primordial sadness.

A few days later Evelyn and I stood on a lot beneath a highway overpass as the car was examined. There is nobody who can love the auto-body man, I thought. Feel gratitude, maybe; but affection, impossible. And after he and the insurance company appraiser had parried and bickered and settled on a cost estimate, and we had returned home in the old family station wagon, the barely healing emotional wounds were opened again.

The auto-body man, upon further investigation, had found more damage to the right side of the car and the door. The telephone conversations that flashed among the insurance people, auto-body man, appraiser, and us dripped with undisguised suspicion. The auto-body man refused to repair the car unless he was paid his full price of $2,623.81.

Solomonic wisdom finally prevailed. It was decided that it was conceivable the right side of the compact sedan had been beaten by the hooves of a large deer. The damage would be covered and the car repaired.

Early on the morning after the accident I had called the police on the notion it was important to have the event recorded on the blotter, and Evelyn had called the house of a family we know where the man is employed by the estate onto which the deer had fled. We wanted the workers to know there might be a wounded buck roaming about, that he might need assistance or protection.

While we awaited the return of the damaged car, Evelyn and I happened into a neighbor who lives two miles from our house. She knew about the accident, but some sense of country discretion dictated that she keep it to herself.

We brought it up. "I know," she said then. "One of the workmen on the estate chased some wild dogs, and one of the dogs dropped the hoof of a deer." She saw our startled faces. "Doesn't mean it was your deer," the woman added hastily. "Lots of deer die in the woods, many of them from natural causes."

A week later, entering our kitchen, which looks out on the woods, I found Evelyn peering out. When she turned I saw that she was crying.

"I bet you're miserable about all the trouble the crash has caused us," I said. She nodded.

"Well, I don't care," I added, and I found myself meaning it. "I only hope that old Two-Six is still out there."

Evelyn smiled. "I love you," she said.

Wood

My wife Evelyn had been opposed to driving the new two-door compact ever since the night it was rammed by a deer when she was at the wheel. I understood, yet I needed the family wagon this day. It was cold and blustery and I'd located a treasure of firewood. Our young daughter already had agreed to come and help gather it. So Evelyn acceded reluctantly, and while our two sons played at a friend's house and my wife departed on her errands, Sara and I headed for the woods.

We drove to a gravel-spread parking area, recently established to accommodate future visitors to the new Rockefeller State Park Preserve. We left the car where the gravel bordered the forest, and began foraging for our prizes among the mounds and valleys of moved earth and stone, hills of sawdust, vines, and timber.

Sara, slim and lithe, excitement lighting her face, virtually pranced over the irregular terrain, locating substantial branches, calling over for my approval, and lugging them back to our wagon. Some were too long or heavy to move, and we used our bow saw to turn these into manageable size. I marveled at Sara's nimbleness and strength. She was, after all, only five years old and forty pounds or less. I began calling to her when I uncovered a usable piece of wood, propping it up for her approval, delighting in her judgment, "That's a beauty, Daddy." I felt a kind of pride and affection that, I suspected, most men, and only lucky ones at that, achieved only with their sons.

When we'd first begun, I'd been concerned about the length and weight of wood Sara was hauling, but she soon assured me she was equal to the task. I couldn't help but think she was also collecting bragging rights for when we were reunited with her seven- and eight-year-old brothers.

It began to snow, but rather than impede us it provided momentum, lent a primeval rightness to what we were doing. We were pleased to be alone; no one else had been bold enough to venture out on this increasingly uncomfortable afternoon, not even with the "Free Wood" sign beckoning from the roadside. After almost two hours we had filled virtually to the top the entire storage area of our suburban wagon and had even piled a handful of logs behind the front seats. Near the end, Sara started to gather increasingly smaller branches, even thick twists of vine masquerading as real wood, revealing both her doggedness and her tiredness. I had begun to grow weary myself.

I thanked Sara profusely for her help. She lowered her lovely brown eyes humbly, and I knew we both could hardly wait to show the rest of the family the oak and maple and hickory that were the fruits of our noble effort.

As we pulled into the driveway and cruised toward the house I noticed the compact was already back in the garage. "Mom's home, Sara, let's show her what we've done," I said. But before Sara could reach the door, my wife was outside, her features contorted.

"I had a crash," she blurted out. "It began to snow and the car in front of me started braking and changing lanes, and it got right in front of me and I couldn't get out of the way. We hit, front to back, and our car got spun around and hit a second time, in the back." When she finished, she was breathless and very sad.

At the time the brand-new compact had collided with the buck, my feelings had tumbled between concern for my wife and concern for my car. This time the feelings were different. I had to admit I was angry at her for again banging up my car. And it occurred that nothing worse than a wayward supermarket shopping cart had ever collided with her station wagon.

I fibbed, feeling the conflict between reason and emotion, and said she was not at any fault in either crash. And I told the truth—that I was very happy she was home safe and sound. "This doesn't mean I'll ask to swap cars again very often," I added, and the coaxing of a small laugh was the balm that began the healing for both of us.

The boys arrived, and Sara took great pleasure in supervising the stacking of the wood. We carried several of the drier pieces in and built a warm and soothing fire. I began to reflect, as fires have a way of making one do.

It had been a remarkable day. I had experienced, with both my wife and daughter, a new and unexpected kind of closeness. And all it had cost was a wracked-up car. I turned to the family gathered in the living room and told them, "No regrets, folks, no regrets." The boys were puzzled. The women knew exactly what I meant.

Vanity

It was late, I was out the door and racing to make the 7:29 to Grand Central, when my boy called from the front step: "Daddy, do I look like you?"

The question triggered such a rush of thoughts and emotions that I stopped in my tracks. I returned to the front door, taking a few extra seconds to compose a reply. "Edward, you look like me a little, but you're more like a movie star or a TV star."

He gave me his smile that, with a tug of the lips and the drop of his ale-brown eyes, can convey shyness and pleasure in one look.

I thought about his question on and off all day. Had someone in school made fun of him? Had a relative delivered some unthinking remark, made some unfavorable comparison, in his presence? Were they talking about his looks? About mine?

It's amazing, I thought, how one forgets the thousands upon thousands of compliments about looks that one has heard from early childhood until a few hours ago, yet remembers with painful clarity the insults.

One evening long ago, when I had exasperated my mother, she turned on me and sputtered, "You ugly duckling." It made me miserable, which I'm sure was her intent. Only later could I realize that it had probably made her just as miserable. And as much as I had explained the moment to myself, there it remained, tucked in my brain, thirty years later.

My mother has fawned over my looks countless times before and after, and I believe that in her eyes I'm one handsome devil. But now the duck and the devil live side by side.

Edward's question made me think of another terrible moment. I was twelve or thirteen, a few years older than he is now, and had gone with some chums to a tough neighborhood in Boston where a grocery store had installed the equivalent of today's video game, the pinball machine.

I was wearing glasses and a knit hat shaped like an aviator's headgear, rendering the wearer not dashing, I soon learned, but possessed of a goofy maroon noggin. One of the slick older local boys spotted me in the crowd around the pinball machine and said to his pal, "Hey, get a load of this kid." That was it. That was all he said. But I felt homely for a long, long time.

At a lunch the day of my son's question I told friends about the episode, for it had become more than a passing question. One told me that his son favored his wife, while his daughter favored him. "She's eight and she's worried," he said. "She asks, 'Dad, when I'm older will I have hair on my chest and under my arms while the hair on top of my head gets thin?'"

It was an easier question to answer than the one lobbed at me. I decided that someone had made a disparaging comment about my looks. When I returned home I broached the subject with my son.

"Edward, why did you ask this morning if you looked like me?"

He became uneasy. "Someone said I did."

"Who, Edward?"

"Just someone."

His reluctance to reveal the source or details of the insult aggravated me. I concluded it must have been a mean companion. I was angry that my boy might be hurt. For myself, I was upset as well. I began to fume over the slight and the damage it might do to Edward's budding self-confidence. I wondered if there had been some odious reference to my mustache or perhaps my, well, generous nose.

Maybe an hour later, in one startling moment, I was struck by a very different thought: what if Edward wants to look exactly like me? I went back to him.

"Edward Salim," I began, using both his first and middle names to signal the importance of the moment, "I've thought it over, and you look a lot like me. Almost exactly like me, except as hard as I try, I can't see your mustache. The same nice smart head and special eyes. My hair is short, but it used to be long and terrific like yours is."

Edward Salim beamed. He was happy, and he was proud to learn that he looked so much like his dad. I had spent a day feeding my misgivings about how handsome or plain or homely I was—about what people perceived when they looked at me.

When Edward was asleep later that night I slipped into his room and approached his bed for another look. He lay with his head to one side, his forehead highlighted in the dimness, his perfect little features serene.

"My son," I said, "how beautiful you are."

The Art of Waving

Trains hurtled by, big trains with bulging locomotives, not far from our house when I was a boy, and the thrill of running down to the tracks and waving to the engineer and getting a wave in return never wore thin.

If we were late and a long freight train was click-clacking by with its geography-lesson collection of cars, we were patient. Chances were, the brakeman would be out on the little platform of his red caboose, and he'd never let a good wave go unnoticed.

For years on end, my family, like millions of other American families, went out for Sunday afternoon automobile rides. Our destination was almost always the same place—the Howard Johnson's near the beach. It didn't take twenty-eight flavors to make me happy. I always ordered either black raspberry or maple walnut in a sugar cone, and they always had one or the other. Besides the ice cream, those Sunday rides were also prime opportunities for waving.

Kids waited atop overpasses, grinning and waving strenuously at strangers, taking pleasure when they got a wave back. You wouldn't drive by a person walking down a country road without a wave, and people who didn't practice this gentle protocol were deemed a little odd.

I didn't think about it much then, but I do now. Waving is one of the great small gestures of mankind. It is the simplest act of animation, the almost effortless raising of an arm and movement of a hand. But what spectacular dividends it can bring!

A wave can stimulate a feeling of warmth, an atmosphere of civility. It can tell people they are attuned to a social order, partners in it, connected to one another, without imposing any unwanted intimacy. Waving is a way for two strangers to tell each other they're both having fun and then move along. Waving communicates between people in a strange land, between infants and grandparents, between all generations.

In more recent years I began to notice that some people were reluctant to wave. During a ride in a speedboat, I waved toward other boats without getting any response. When we cruised slowly through a channel back to the dock I tried again, waving to other boaters and people on the banks. They looked away. I was disappointed and puzzled.

I saw some people standing on an overpass not so long ago, and when I waved, I got a glare in return. I drove behind a station wagon brimming with children. They were huddled in the outback, behind the seats. The motion of the car tumbled them gently about, like playful cubs. I waved. They did nothing. I figured they couldn't see through the glare of the glass, so I waved again. They finally saw me. The startled cubs turned toward the front of the wagon and reported me to their parents.

I began to feel that a small but important practice was being lost. I also had an inspiration.

I rounded up my children—although one may borrow someone else's children, or go alone, or take the grandchildren—and we headed down to the local railroad station.

We didn't pay much attention to the electrified commuter trains, with their drivers sealed off in little compartments. We waited for an old diesel locomotive, fat and wide, to come hauling its train down the tracks.

When it approached, we began waving. The engineer leaned out of the high side window of his cab, spotted us and began waving back. As he got closer he waved harder, then reached back in and blew a handful of blasts on his whistle. As he passed I saw the pleasure on his face, as he must have seen it on mine. We waved to each other until he was gone, a quarter-mile beyond the station.

The children were so ecstatic they jumped up and down. They hugged each other and danced around the platform. Inside, I did the same.

Trains

How wrong the kindly man in the store had been. "See you the day after Christmas," he said. "You'll be in with your boys for more track. Happens every time."

After a half-hour of looking, aisle-side interviews with other customers and discussions with clerks, my wife Evelyn and I picked out a spectacular-looking electric train set.

"Last one in the store," said the manager. "HO size. More versatile than the other ones. And less expensive when you start expanding." It was in a box with a cellophane lid so that the locomotive and all the cars were visible. I had wanted to buy the Amtrak set, arguing that was the train the children waved to as it sped up and down the Hudson Division tracks not far from our home.

"Freight train's the best," said the kindly clerk. "This for your boys? Well, they go for the freight train every time."

His words sparked a reverie, back to when I was a young boy and was fascinated by the trains that ran near our home. The man was right on that score. My friends and I just about ignored the passenger trains. The only one I cared about was the one that carried my dad home at night. But we loved the freight trains. We loved counting the number of cars and waiting for the caboose to flash by so we could wave to the man on the platform and get him to wave back. We happen to be a family of wavers.

"Freight train it is," I said happily. My wife and I could feel our excitement rising. I lugged the huge box to the front of the store, paid and we thanked the man for his help. "Enjoy them," he said. "And don't forget what I said. See you the day after Christmas."

Our two sons, Edward and Charles, ages eleven and ten, pulled back the wrapping on the great mysterious box on Christmas morning, set up the tracks in their large bedroom at my coaxing and lay on their stomachs operating the train from the transformer switch for several minutes. But they exhibited growing impatience when the locomotive, the old-fashioned steam locomotive that had its own headlamp and puffed smoke, sometimes jumped the track. In less time than it took to select the trains, they fled their bedroom for more satisfying gifts downstairs.

Our daughter Sara, who is eight, and I were left to play with the first electric train set our family, including me, had ever owned. My girl seemed to enjoy them enough, I couldn't tell if part of her enthusiasm had to do with instinctively soothing her dad. I loved her for it but began to feel forlorn.

The trains had cost almost $150. I considered the sum a small fortune, and it was the most expensive item anyone had bought for anyone else in our family for as long as we had been exchanging Christmas and Chanukah presents. Evelyn shared in my puzzlement, if not my exasperation. "Let's leave it set up," she suggested. "Perhaps the boys will become interested after the initial excitement of Christmas is over." It was a wise and thoughtful notion, but it did not prove to be an accurate one.

I entered the boys' room a week later to find the set in disarray— the tank cars, coal cars, box cars, the caboose either on their sides or sitting on separated tracks to nowhere; the transformer, counter to the warning in the instruction booklet, still plugged in but obviously ignored.

I raised my voice in—what?—anger, annoyance, disappointment? The boys responded by disassembling the set, fitting each car into its original little box, and arranging the boxes on an open shelf.

I returned to the room one day months later, when the house was empty and I was supposed to be writing. The train boxes were coated with dust. Lint hung from a few pieces of track that they had not been able to repack. They were, I thought, miniature versions of the rusty tracks no train runs on anymore.

The boys had refused to speculate about what deserving family or community group would appreciate the trains, and I realized now the vindictive hurt that had been embedded in my question. I looked at my watch, shrugged and began to unpack the trains for myself. I got the figure-eight arrangement assembled, and then set up the entire train on the tracks, behind the locomotive and its coal tender. I plugged in the transformer, lay on the floor, pulled the switch carefully to the right and off it went.

The great ten-car, multi-colored freight train headed down the track, crossed the first spur, and took me back to my childhood. What great fun! I pulled the train to a halt, backed her up, adjusted the wheels on the mighty locomotive, and set out again. After a while I'd had my fill for the day, and put the train set away.

By then I knew exactly what had happened. I remembered that kids never forget important things. I had wanted a set of electric trains for almost forty years and had finally gotten them. My boys had wanted them when they were five and six years old. I had said no, concerned for their safety. Forgive me, my boys, in my fun. When you want the trains back, twenty or thirty years from now, it won't be easy, but you've got my word. I promise to hand them over.

Fig Newtons and Crab Apples

Dear Mrs. Saperstein:

I bet you're surprised to hear from me after all these years. I intended to write before, then I forgot. But as you can see from this letter, I never really forgot. They used to say I was the "stubbornest" kid in our neighborhood. I haven't changed. It wasn't easy to find you and being stubborn helped. I hope you're well. My parents are all right; you know, they're growing old. My wife and I have two boys and a girl. We feel blessed by them. My oldest boy, Edward, is going to be eight years old, the same age as your Martin when we last saw each other. I look at my son sometimes and I see my old friend Martin. That's the main reason for this letter. I imagine you once had a thousand questions, and I was not very helpful to you. By harking back to those days, maybe I can give you some answers now.

The only reason we didn't play outside your house was that the trains that crossed the trestle just below your house left the air sooty. I don't mean to insult your old house. Our triple-decker was no bargain. We had mice. I think they were rats, but my parents didn't want to make me even more frightened. We had trouble getting heat. My mother was afraid the super would beat up my father if he complained. The super owned the house and lived on the first floor. He was a big ex-marine, and the word around the neighborhood was that the marines sent him home because the service had made him crazy.

Even so, everything seemed a little cleaner and greener around our place. We had the vacant lot across the street, where trees had taken hold, and the old horse chestnut trees along the sidewalks. Some of the other houses on my block had hedges out front, and there were rose bushes that kept us from reaching the crab apples in Mrs. Sullivan's front yard.

That explains why I liked my block better than yours, but Martin and I rarely played down my way, either. Once in a while we went over to the field they flooded in winter for skating. I don't know how much Martin ever told you about how we spent our time after school. I guess that was some of the information you wanted when you asked me in for the cookies and milk so long ago. I remember you and the snack and the kitchen table clearly.

Well, we disliked the trestle but our specialty was the railroads. We usually spent part of our afternoons on the footbridge near Arbutus Avenue waiting for a train to come through. We'd wait a half-hour or even an hour if we had to. When we spotted the locomotive we always ducked down to avoid the black smoke. Once the locomotive passed, we leaped up and tried to figure out the length of the train. Sometimes we counted the cars—one of us the box cars, the other the tank cars—but we really wanted to see the red caboose. We hoped there was a trainman outside, and when there was we ran to the other side of the footbridge and shouted and waved. And the trainman waved back every time. We believed he shouted, too, but it was too noisy to hear. We loved that moment. Martin said he was going to ask his dad for a denim engineer's cap for his birthday. I was going to ask my family for one, and we were going to wear them on the footbridge. I never got mine; I don't know about Martin.

When it was very cold or raining, Martin and I didn't wait on the footbridge. We crossed over it and went to the donut shop on Norfolk Street, where you could see the donut machine in the window. It dropped dough like yellow smoke rings into the bubbling oil, and in a few moments golden donuts bounced up to the surface. They cost a nickel, seven cents if the man spread chocolate over the top. Once in a while Martin and I saved our nickels and went to the soda fountain on the next corner. There we played the gumball machine, hoping to win some prize like a ring or the dice.

On the way home we went by Mr. Batchelder's grocery store and then out to our own street, where we parted in time for supper. We didn't enter Mr. Batchelder's store very much. Do you remember him? He was old and large behind that blue apron, with his walrus mustache and calabash pipe. He smoked Edgeworth Ready-Rubbed, and the store reeked of it. I loved the smell and never forgot it. I smoked it for a while when I grew up, though I gave up smoking entirely twelve years ago. Even now, coming off the commuter train at night, I may get a whiff of that Edgeworth, like sweet, wet wood, and I feel like going up to the smoker and telling him of my pleasure. It's only smoke and smell, but it gives me a sense of order, even belonging. It helps me understand where I've been and where I'm going. But let me tell you about Mr. Batchelder. Martin and I noticed that his shelves were poorly stocked—a few cans of peas, a few boxes of tea, the pipe tobacco—and we decided that when they were all sold Mr. Batchelder would die. So we stopped going in, because we were scared and because by staying away we felt we were helping to keep him alive.

As much as we enjoyed the footbridge, sometimes Martin and I used the dirt path near Mr. Batchelder's that led directly to the railroad tracks. You could cross over them and come out on Norfolk. The dirt path served as a stop for the trains out of South Station bound for the South Shore and Cape Cod. After supper in the warm weather we returned to the path and waited for the train to stop and let off the men returning home from work in town. My dad was one of them, and I loved seeing him appear from under the dark arbor and the bright steam. He smiled and took my hand and we walked home together. I suppose I was so happy I don't remember ever seeing Martin's dad.

That was pretty much our pattern, Mrs. Saperstein. It may not sound like much now, but we were very happy doing our "railroading" and the time flew by. Once in a while we picked up stones from the rail bed and practiced pitching, but I swear we didn't aim at lamps or passing trains or people or even each other. If you asked me about cats and dogs, I couldn't guarantee we were innocent.

There were eight tracks at that stretch of the line, and I suppose we took our chances crossing, but we had a lot of respect for those trains, and we were extremely cautious. Once or twice we got caught on an embankment as a train came rolling through, and we crouched in the stones and weeds and felt the ground beneath us shake. Those trains taught respect.

No reflection on you, but Martin was on the skinny side, and he had that cotton batting in his ears. I remember that because it saved him from the tough kids in the neighborhood. Did you happen to read the story that the Jewish people owed the Irish people a great debt? It was a wonderful story. It said that abuse by the Irish on the street toughened the Jewish children physically, and the devoted Irish teachers in the public schools toughened them mentally. I think that was true. No one picked on Martin because he did seem frail, but I was the wise guy. It was that stubborn streak. My mother said, "Don't wear your yarmulke in the street; they'll taunt you; they'll beat you." But I decided to taunt them. I became the holy man—well, the holy boy—and walked home from Hebrew school with my head high and my black yarmulke on top of it. And it worked. They were amazed. They asked themselves, Where does this kid get the nerve to wear that cap? I frustrated them until they hollered, "Hey, Jewball! Take off your cap and fight fair!" Honest to God, it was terrific.

Don't get me wrong about the Irish. Some were my good friends. I even walked with them to Saint Matthew's Church on Saturdays and waited outside while they did whatever they had to do inside. And this may surprise you—I married an Irish girl, an Irish American girl. The first time I brought her home my mother took me aside in the kitchen and said, "She's very nice. Never bring her here again." But my mother fell in love with her shortly after I did, and one day when we visited my mom slipped her diamond ring off and put it on the hand of my wife-to-be.

Back to Martin and me and the railroads. Our other favorite spot was down by the coal and coke silo. Strung across those train yards were what looked like rows of leather strips. A man who drove a coal truck told us that when railroad men riding atop the cars entered the yards at night they got slapped by the leather strips so they'd know where they were. It seemed like a rude and painful way to find out, and we never really believed him. We saw our first snake down by those yards. It came out of field and onto the street, green and black, a garter snake, and we were fascinated. Martin and I were sure it would get squashed by a passing truck, but we were afraid to pick it up and return it to the weeds. For a long time we examined that spot every time we passed, looking for clues, but we never found out about the snake.

One day when I came in for supper I found my mother in a strange and frightening state. She was sickly pale. She grabbed me in a hug, then pushed me away and studied my face. She began to cry, then clenched her fists to make the tears stop. When she finally spoke, her voice was so soft that it made the moment that much more terrifying. "Were you with him?" she asked. When I didn't answer she repeated the words exactly the same way. I finally said, "Martin?" and answered with a nod and a shudder. I told her that Martin and I had gone to the footbridge and returned home by Mr. Batchelder's and that I'd left him at the corner of our street.

Our house was awfully silent. I was fed supper and told not to go out to wait for my father that evening. The trains were tied up for several hours, and he got home long after dark.

I was nervous but I came to your apartment a few days later for Fig Newtons and milk, as you asked me to. I remember the way you sat at the table in your apron, with your sad and pretty face propped in your hands, asking a lot of questions. I know you wondered why I suddenly stopped showing up. I felt ashamed, but I had to.

After I disappeared from your block, I spent most of my free time at the other end of the street, near home, and didn't go near the railroads, except to meet my dad. That summer I figured out a way around the rose bushes in front of Mrs. Sullivan's and got my first taste of her crab apples. They were sour, but after all that effort I pretended that they were delicious.

At first I didn't believe the kids on the street when they said that Martin was hard of hearing. I had spent all that time with him, and he'd fooled me. I'll never know why he climbed up to the trestle because we were frightened to go near there. I know it doesn't count but I've thought over the years—if I'd been with him, I would have heard the train in time.

I wrote this letter to let you know that Martin was a wonderful friend. I also wanted to say that you were kind and generous to me and how sorry I was to desert you when you needed to have me around. I know you didn't blame me for Martin, but I got scared when you stopped asking about him and began talking about me. Even then, Mrs. Saperstein, I understood what you wanted, but I couldn't replace Martin, I just couldn't become your little boy.

Sincerely,

Herbie

Bedtime Tales

You don't have to read this whole story to find out the moral. The moral of the story is: when the salesman says your beds will be delivered in three weeks, it's a lot of bunk.

If you're captivated by bedtime tales, here's the rest of what happened.

The boys were ecstatic. They were picking out their own bunk bed in the big store in White Plains, New York. Three weeks, said the salesman sullenly, a mood I mistook for sincerity.

We paid for the beds over the Memorial Day weekend and spent the better part of four months awaiting delivery.

During the wait, the big store even put the same beds on sale. I read them (1) the ad and (2) the Riot Act, and they sent a check for the difference. But no beds arrived.

The boys' initial joy turned to wrath. In fact, we spent the summer taking turns composing the most heinous diatribes against the big store and its salesman.

In our spare time we visited other stores, hoping to find bunk beds to replace the ones that apparently were still attached to trees in North Carolina.

A procession of summer visitors found themselves bivouacking in various parts of the house instead of enjoying their slumber in the beds the bunks were meant to replace.

Periodically, we would call a collection of numbers associated with the big store, but no matter whom we spoke with, the blame always lay elsewhere. The most often-used excuse had to do with a backlog in Minnesota. I told them I liked my oak log in North Carolina explanation better.

After a few months we began to get a series of promising telephone calls. One was to verify our order, another to confirm our address and get precise directions, still another to extract the promise that we would be at home on a particular day.

With some trepidation, we told our boys the beds might be installed about the time they returned to school. They breathed astonishingly elaborate threats against the store in case this was yet another sham.

The day of deliverance came, with the hope in the household falling as the sun edged farther and farther west. But the truck came. There was a moment of delirium.

Only a moment. These employees explained that they only delivered. Another specialist would have to be booked for assembling. The boys gnashed their teeth and fell to the floor. My wife Evelyn and I stared at two huge boxes.

"Good excuse for a Martini," I said.

"Bring the white wine while you're at it," she replied.

Many calls later it was arranged for the assembler to visit. He apparently worked in mysterious ways, for no one could tell us what time he would actually appear. We established our vigil on the appointed day. At 1:45 PM, a school crisis forced us to abandon the house. We wrote a hasty note to the assembler, promising to be back by 3:00 PM, tops.

We were back at 2:25 PM. The assembler had snatched our note and left a chilling card ordering us not to contact the big store but to wait silently until it decided to reach us.

We called anyhow and were told the assembler could not return for ten or more days. The assembler was punishing us, it seemed, for leaving the house.

We dallied with the notion of putting the beds together ourselves, but harked back to the saga of the Yugoslav bentwood rocker. It was bought in a box one day many years ago from a salesman—this one smiled too much, so beware of both smiling and sullen salesmen—who said assembly required only one screwdriver. It took us a week, and it would have taken longer had we not disregarded the instructions and attacked the parts based on instinct. The instructions had been printed in two tongues—the first in what we guessed was Serbo-Croatian and, for the export trade, some language that most closely resembled the sounds made by apes at the zoo when you laugh at them.

In the matter of the bunks, more days and nights passed. Upon arrival home one evening, I repeated the resolve I'd earlier stated over the telephone: we would not sleep until we built those bunk beds. "I'll pour while you go upstairs and get the instructions out of the boxes," I said to Evelyn.

She was back in ten minutes. "They've outdone the Yugoslavs," she said. "There are slats and posts and boards and all kinds of nuts and bolts, and no instructions at all."

The next morning we pleaded for the mercy of the manager of the big store, and a few days after that the assembler who had fled our house earlier appeared on our doorstep.

Familiar with the endless and tawdry drama culminating with his efforts, he eschewed endearing chitchat and went right to work. The boys and I watched the beds take shape. In thirty or forty minutes, he was done.

The assembler packed his toolbox to leave, but I intercepted him. He seemed startled.

"This is a great day for us," I began, turning to look at the magnificent oak monument he had erected, "and someone has to be rewarded. The only question is, who? Shall it be the salesman, the store manager, the delivery people, or you?"

The assembler peered around uncomfortably, as if expecting he might momentarily learn he was on *Candid Camera*.

"Me, I guess," he said, when no hoax became revealed.

I pressed a twenty-dollar bill into his screwdriver hand. As he fled, the assembler's face flickered in a comical balance between dark confusion and bright gratitude. He couldn't figure out our behavior. He would have to sleep on it.

The Civics Lesson

Pulling open the door of the barbershop, I was relieved to find it almost empty. I led my two young sons to a bench and pointed out a pile of magazines and tabloid newspapers they could browse through. In the barber's chair a stout, middle-aged man with neat graying hair sat awaiting a haircut, and slouched in the second chair a youngish policeman watched a boxing match on a small black-and-white television set mounted in a corner near the ceiling. For no good reason, I liked the back of the head of the man who wanted a haircut and disliked the back of the head of the policeman.

The barber reentered the room. I guessed he had gone to call his bookmaker, only because I heard him speaking into a telephone in the next room and because I've always considered barbershops fascinating and raffish. Both my boys were so long overdue for trims that they had agreed to be brought in without their usual complaints and whimpers about how the barber and I were going to conspire to wreck their perfect hair styles as well as undermine their gender and their senses of independence. Pleasantly mystified as I was by the barber and his operation, he must have been more so about me, for I never got a haircut myself—just the children—yet appeared somewhat civilized, if not chic, about the head. The explanation is that my haircuts for the past several years have been self-inflicted at the bathroom mirror, with a little plastic device that accepts a double-edged razor blade and permits the user to create, depending on his luck and skill, either a modish haircut or tonsorial bedlam. Fussing over my dark hair and mustache, at times I had accomplished both.

It was important that the shop should not be busy, for in just one hour I was due on my job. The barber—one barber, guaranteed waiting—had done careful, thoughtful haircuts on the boys before, and we had begun to trust him. Once he had annoyed me by complaining that the chlorine in one boy's hair—I'd picked him up at the local swimming pool—was making his job particularly difficult. "Are you saying you don't want to cut his hair?" I asked. The cop, of course, that's why I didn't like him, was there that time, on duty, I suspected, and neglecting his job of maintaining safety at his intersection nearby. He shot up in his seat and spun around, a foolish and melodramatic response to imagined danger. But the barber was pacifying. "No, no, I'll do it, but it's better without the chlorine," which was satisfactory to me. Today both boys, they are nine and ten, had freshly shampooed heads.

The middle-aged customer was briskly served and, after an exchange of small talk, money, and thank you's, was gone. My younger son went first, up on the special flat saddle for children of his size, and I checked my watch, leaned back and relaxed. I liked this place, appreciated that the girlie magazines were kept on a high shelf out of sight of the children. The room had a nice, small-town feel, like the barbershop I'd visited each month as a youngster. The grownups might say things to each other a boy wasn't expected to understand, but he was an accepted member of the barbershop fraternity. My boys were there for the same reason as the adults, amid the jars that were alleged to sterilize scissors and combs; the automatic shaving-foam dispenser; the masculine powders, lotions, and smells; and the expanse of mirror with the cherished family photos taped along the edges; the price list in the Woolworth's frame, and the old-fashioned ornamental cash register. The boys understood that one day the barber would lean close to them, and they would smile and appreciate all the whispered jokes and intimate words that are spoken between men in only a few specials places.

The barber tucked in my son, indulged in brief discussion with both him and me on the kind of haircut desired, and began his industrious snipping. The policeman was virtually motionless in the other chair. My elder son sat next to me, alternately turning magazine pages, watching TV, and casually taking in the room. I peered up at the TV set but found the boxing action unexciting and delved into an outdated copy of *People*.

"Kill the nigger," the barber said. The magazine fell to my lap, and my head snapped up. The barber nodded toward the TV set and smiled at me. It was clear that he expected I would enjoy his comment. The policeman didn't budge. I glared at the barber. My look was meant to convey, "What are you saying to me? What do you know about me? How dare you try to poison my little boys!" He seemed not to notice. For a moment, I practiced announcing a lie, in order to shame him, that he had offended my race. I don't know why I didn't. Was it the slouching cop, embarrassment for the barber, concern that the haircuts would not be done that day, or was it the plain, cold fear of confrontation?

Both haircuts were completed, and the barber was paid, including his standard tip. We returned home without mention of the remark. As we drove I thought back to when my wife and I were new to the suburbs. A family on the block had invited us over for beer and cheese and crackers and to meet a few other neighbors. After we all were cozy one of them said: "I bet you're glad to be in this neighborhood. Nobody has to worry about blacks around here." I lied, replying, "Don't be so sure. I am partly black myself." Despite this inauspicious first meeting, we are these several years later good friends. But about the barber's comment, I said nothing, and it soon became clear that I, not the barber, was suffering disgrace. I remembered another story, one that would have been long forgotten had not the storyteller, a member of my family, repeated it a half-dozen times over the past few decades and had not his son continued to laugh at the retelling.

The man and his son, then about seven, were walking down a main street of their middle-class hometown when they came upon a young black man. The boy pointed his hand toward the stranger and burst into a fit of laughter. In the youngster's defense, it must be said he had never before really noticed differences in people's color. His father, stepping back to view exactly what was happening, burst into laughter himself. The black man hung his head and walked away. The story is part of the reason I have never been able to like either the man, who is now in his advanced years, or the boy, who in the realm of tolerance, has become the same man as his father.

At home, the boys brought up the barber's remark. "He was stupid, Dad," said Edward. "In the first place, both fighters were black."

"I know," I said, "But did you see the way I glared at him?"

The glare had not registered with either son. I was fooling myself. I had not had the guts to get up and denounce the utterer of that vile slur, snatch up my half-shorn son, and toss a glance of contempt at the cop as I fled the shop. Or even beckon the barber from his chores and explain in a barbershop whisper: I like blacks as much as any other kind of people, and I want my sons, as well as my daughter, whose bangs you have trimmed, to grow up feeling the same way. Even though you may feel your remark was harmless, never speak that way in front of us again.

Instead, I learned anew in the barbershop a terrible thing. I learned how vulnerable to bigotry I am. I learned that the barber with an offhand remark had paralyzed me into silence and confused my children.

After much mental rehearsing, I called the boys together a day later and made a difficult speech. "I know how much you love your Irish grandma. And you would be very upset if someone tried to hurt her. Well, when Mom's mother came to America as a young woman, some people called her bad names." I told them the names, and they looked startled. "I'm not making it up. And my parents, Nanny and Grandpa. When I was a little boy they were called terrible things right in front of me. Some people hated them without even knowing them because they are Jews. You know how proud Grandpa is of his Syrian heritage. They found out about that, and he got it double." I told them the names.

Their beautiful little mouths fell open. "Boys, when a person's race is insulted, or his religion, or the country his family came from, you have only two real choices. You can join the insulter, or you can defend the victim. I hope you will never join the insulter."

They nodded never.

"So if someone talks like that barber did, I want you to do what I couldn't quite do. I want you to say with pride: 'Mister, my mom and dad, my sister and brother and I, we are all niggers.'"

When I had finished they looked at me and at each other and nodded that they believed they understood, but I knew it wasn't that easy. I also knew that at night in their bunk beds they would think about it and talk about it between themselves. They're good boys, and before long they'll get the idea.

Shame

The window of the shop on Bedford Road in Pleasantville, New York, has long been repaired, but the inside remains empty.

One night about a year ago, a brick or large stone was hurled through the window. Attached to it was a note expressing hate for Jews. Reading the story in the local paper I, like many other people, felt anger and sadness. More than fifty years later, someone had celebrated his own Kristallnacht.

I was not a customer of the shop, which offered gourmet food, except for an occasional non-gourmet item, like a bag of bagels. But I put my three young children in the car and we drove the three miles to Pleasantville and parked in the municipal lot between the store and the new church. When we entered, the burly young proprietor, apron pulled across his waist in the age-old custom of the food merchant, stared at us from behind the counter waiting for our order. "We're here to say we're very sorry about what happened," I told him.

He was surprised. "How did you find out?" he asked. He peered down at the children and for some reason looked ashamed.

"It was in the newspaper. We feel very bad about it. If there's anything we can do for you, please let us know."

His manner softened and he said, "Thank you, thank you very much."

I saw in his eyes that he wanted to know if I were a Jew. That made me examine my feelings. Would I have made the trip to his shop if I were not a Jew? For him and for me, I wanted to believe people would, so I didn't acknowledge his look. We said good-bye and left without buying anything. I felt it was extremely important for the children to know that something bad had happened, though on the way home I had a hard time telling them why.

In the following weeks I looked for the next story, the one providing reassuring information, describing the arrest, explaining the act away as the prank of juvenile vandals. I asked at the barbershop across the street where the policeman takes his break in the spare chair. No one had heard anything. One day I drove by and the shop was empty. I don't know if the shop was doing poorly because of customers like me or if the proprietor was tired of the long hours or if he was sick in his heart.

Two swastikas were painted outside the office of the Young Men's and Young Women's Hebrew Association on Tompkins Avenue in Pleasantville about the time the recent Jewish New Year observance concluded. The office is a couple of hundred feet from where the man used to operate his food shop. This latest incident was kept secret for five days.

Officials said they had first wanted to discuss it with Jewish community leaders. They said they had not wanted to impede the police investigation. The village board of trustees finally issued a press release condemning the vandalism. Several people lied to the local paper, saying it was terrible but the first time such a thing had happened.

Had the shopkeeper suffered his fear and outrage and indignity for nothing? Give me a better answer. Give a better one to my children.

The Flag

When I was very young, I learned to love the flag. It and free ice cream were waved in front of one's nose on the Fourth of July. No one had to pretend to listen to the politicians once the ice cream was passed around.

A few years later, there were parades. Strong grim men, back from over there, marched down the avenue behind columns of flags. Women, happy and crying, waved handkerchiefs. Beneath them, on the curb, we children had small flags on sticks and kept shaking them back and forth. The soldiers weren't supposed to turn their heads and look around, but some of them did. We made them smile. Some of them cried, too.

About the same time a picture became famous. It showed a small bunch of U.S. Marines raising the flag at a placed called Iwo Jima. Everyone loved the picture, even though it was posed. It was the re-enactment of what had already happened. It made no difference, though, for the picture of the marines and their flag made a whole country proud.

But after the war something strange happened. Certain people and causes seized the flag and called it their own. And if you disagreed with their point of view, you weren't against only them, you were against the flag. Since they wore the flag, they hid behind it, wrapped themselves in it; they prevented people with other beliefs from enjoying the flag.

It was crazy, but this trick worked. I stopped feeling close to the flag and felt, as I grew older, that the flag did not and would never again mean what it used to. When I saw a flag on a front lawn or raised diagonally on a pole outside a front door, I started saying sarcastically, "Look at that. Must be Americans living inside." Deep down, I was really angry that the flag had been taken away from me.

Then came the bicentennial. Evelyn and I were newly installed in our first house. The two hundredth anniversary of victory over tyranny and the founding of our country transcended anything else I thought the flag had come to stand for. We bought a beauty, measuring four feet by six, and up it went.

The Americans with the flag on their front lawn ambled over and delivered a lecture on flag etiquette, warning that the flag had to be taken in at nightfall and whenever it rained. Arriving home during more than one cloudburst, I noticed that they had ignored their own standards. I also realized how dumb it was to let these people or anyone else usurp my pleasures over the flag.

Iranian zealots captured the U.S. embassy in Tehran and the Americans in it. Up went my flag. It would stay up, night and day, until we had our people home. Pictures of the flag became famous again, only this time they showed Iranians throwing the flag to the ground and burning it. I shook with rage. "Have your revolution," I hollered, "but do not destroy my flag!"

Our family, which by then had grown to include three children, moved to a house set back in the woods. The flag remained folded in a storage box, but as Memorial Day weekend approached, I found it. I figured out a way to unfurl it between two trees at roadside and was pleased to see it every time I returned home. I even got in the habit of placing my right hand over my heart, the way some of the men did at the old parades while others removed their hats as the flag went by.

Before I could get around to taking the flag down, Flag Day was on the calendar. And then, I reasoned, it didn't make much sense to remove the flag just to put it back out a few weeks later.

The children wanted to know why the flag was flying. "It's to remember all the soldiers and sailors who had to die in wars to keep our country free from bad people, people who wanted to push us around and make us sad," I told them. "It's a way of saying you're happy to be American."

They looked at each other and back at me. I'll explain it again on the Fourth of July. This time with ice cream.

Patriotism

Sudden rain washed out the parade to the school and the wreath-laying at the two bronze tablets set in boulders on the front lawn. Families ran through the downpour, hunched and squinting, to the meeting hall at the firehouse. Inside, children scampered down the corridors as their parents secured folding chairs for the big ceremony.

Mr. and Mrs. David Rockefeller arrived from their nearby estate. Their appearance sparked excitement and buzzing and furtive examinations. Both wore warm expressions on their faces. Mr. Rockefeller, the guest speaker, was dressed in a well-fitting grey suit, somewhat rumpled. His brown shoes were not freshly shined. He carried himself confidently but with seeming effort, a man balanced between middle and old age. His wife, dressed in dark hues, looked pretty and unpretentious. The Rockefellers took their seats at the window side of the hall, and the ceremony began.

In marched the local contingents of Brownies and Boy Scouts and the school band. Then came the volunteer fire department in dress blues. All but one lined up at the wall opposite the guest speaker and his wife. The last, a young, handicapped man, made his way into the room with the aid of two aluminum crutches. It took several minutes for him to reach his comrades. He sported a blond mustache and wore glasses. He wore the same fireman's outfit, though one point of his white collar pointed skyward and his pillbox cap was tilted until it almost covered one eye.

The fire company stood at attention until its ranks were complete. Then the men took their seats. Once again, the maneuver took the fireman in the last seat painstaking extra time.

The Brownies and the Boy Scouts performed their rites, at once wholesome and familiar yet vaguely secretive.

The school band played the anthem and several martial airs that the audience seemed not to recognize. Someone whispered that the bandmaster had planned it that way rather than conduct old favorites poorly and risk the scorn of the listeners.

Mr. Rockefeller was introduced. He rose, notes in hand. "Friends and neighbors," he began.

By then the children felt restive, confined by the rain, anxious for the refreshments. The adults remained attentive. Several men wore stylish wool jackets and ties; others had flannel shirts, the collars open to reveal tough hides of neck. Most of the women dressed simply; some had on jeans.

Mr. Rockefeller warned of the "tyranny of the left and the right" and said that "global dialogue" must replace "fisticuffs and missiles." He said that terrorism of every stripe had to be condemned. He asked remembrances for the men and women who did not return from the wars. He called the observance "Decoration Day" instead of Memorial Day.

Everyone applauded. He looked pleased. The audience was asked to rise for the playing of Taps. Mournful bugle sounds came from the hallway behind the auditorium, played by a schoolboy of Korean ancestry. His father who was in a coma, the apparent victim of a hit-and-run accident near his house, would die a short time later.

Mr. Rockefeller stood with the rest and placed his right hand over his heart. Directly across from him, the handicapped firefighter struggled up, leaning his stronger arm on a crutch. When he was finally on his feet, his left arm shot up to his forehead in a proud salute.

Refreshments were served. I finished pouring coffee from a large metal urn as Mr. Rockefeller approached. We shook hands and spoke for a moment. When he stepped away, ten men and women rushed in toward me to fill the space, like seawater finding a new depression in the sand. They wanted to know every word. "I said to him, 'David, I have this new idea and I've been thinking a joint venture might be in order ...'"

They looked at me in disbelief, so I said the real words. "'Good to meet you, I enjoyed your talk,' I told him. 'Nice to meet you. Thanks for coming,' he answered." My friends and neighbors weighed and sifted the words, looking as if they wished they had participated in the momentous exchange.

Driving home through the pelting rain I glanced over at the tablets on the school lawn and, despite myself, burst into tears. "Aah, Dad, it's been a big morning, hasn't it?" said my wife, "Rockefeller and the parade music and the ceremony and all."

"It was the snap of that poor fireman's wrist," I told her. "That salute told me everything about patriotism I ever hope to know."

Gold Stars

The thirty-five cents included five pennies, and I kept poking my hand into my pants pocket to count the coins again and again as I made the walk by myself from home to the five-and-ten, a mile and a half away. It was the first time I was doing my own Christmas shopping.

I don't know how long I spent in the store, though I have the feeling the sales ladies were very patient with me. I was seven. When I finally headed home with my choices, I was certain I had gotten, for the price, the most wonderful little gifts possible. On Christmas I presented my mother with a silver-colored thimble, my father with a white handkerchief, and my sister with a hair ribbon. My brother was not yet born.

We listened to Bing Crosby sing "White Christmas" on the console radio in the living room and spent a lot of time looking out the window to see if snow would cover the cold, dark gray of the streets. Then we went back to the radio, which seemed to feature another man singing, "I'd like to get you, on a slow boat to China." I knew from talk in the household and out on the streets, and from the disappearance of some of the younger grown-ups from the neighborhood, that a war was going on.

When the snow came, it meant business. We children spent what seemed like the entire Christmas vacation and weeks afterward digging snow tunnels and igloos that no car or truck could damage. They simply used the one open lane of our street or stayed away altogether.

Mrs. Courtney, who lived in a house behind ours with several grown sons, saw me dressed up for the holidays, rushed out, and stuffed a dollar bill into my breast pocket. She was very large, and smiling. Later, my mother, almost in tears, conveyed how generous her gesture was.

Next door, I visited the Manna family, who had two small boys. A grandmother and grandfather living with them seemed to work full-time—cooking, baking, cleaning, repairing, he making furniture, both of them gardening and farming on their large plot in the warm weather. Not much later, that grandpa in a shiny wooden coffin in the Manna living room was the first dead body I saw. The boys and I exchanged presents. It was an exchange rather than just a taking because of my parents' thoughtfulness. I remember everyone but can't remember anything I received that year for Christmas.

Christmas fever began building in my current household in early November. The three children, the oldest six years, showed remarkable reserve in their demands. I was partly responsible because every time I saw a television commercial for a toy, I leaped up and shouted, "I want that, oh, I must have that, and I'll die if I don't get it!" I called it instruction in discretionary consumption.

My wife Evelyn and I listened carefully to the requests most often repeated, weighing whether the gifts were suitable and affordable.

Edward Salim created a paper Christmas tree at school and taped it up on a prominent spot at the foot of the cellar stairs. It became our first holiday decoration, though it looked suspiciously like a point-of-purchase display. Edward, who did not seem to harbor any theatrical ambitions, began singing "Jingle Bells," accompanied with an extraordinary bit of his own choreography. Just as he launched into the last line—"Oh, what fun it is …"—he raced across the living room and leaped onto the sofa, finishing with his arms thrust out in jubilation.

Charles Aram, who is five, did not present us with a parade of present requests, but we sensed that behind those large, contemplative brown eyes was the ardent wish they be not just clothes.

Sara Jameela, the proverbial three going on twenty-five, did not make any special demands either but did make it clear that she would commandeer and requisition every gift in the house unless she got her fair share. Strange thing is she has such a sweet, subliminal way of telling us.

Maybe it's Christmas and maybe it's growing up, but all three children began following me around, wanting to help carry in wood, sweep the floor, make repairs at the work bench, rake late leaves (for a little while), even help prepare dinners.

When it came time to decorate the outside of our home, the children and I strode into the woods and snipped hefty sprigs of pine and hemlock and balsam to make our wreath. Evelyn added a red ribbon, and we attached it near the front door, as fragrant and pleasing and ordinary as it could be.

But that wreath is what makes Christmas for my children different from the Christmases of my early memory. Some houses may have had wreaths back then, but many others had blue satin scrolls with a gold star in the middle hung in the window. It meant a very sad Christmas inside. Some scrolls had two gold stars. I don't know how those houses got by. It makes every Christmas without them merry.

Franklin Field

Most people have a favorite field. It might be a lot filled with goldenrod and chokeberry near the house where you were a child, or a campus green, or a meadow in the mountains where you confessed to love. Mine is Franklin Field. Not the famous stadium in Philadelphia but the stretch of turf and dust, jagged at one end and more than a half-mile long, in the Dorchester section of Boston, Massachusetts. Over the last few decades, the joy and anger and hope of shifting populations have played out in Franklin Field. It is my favorite because it was there, during hundreds of visits over several youthful years, that I learned many important things.

The biggest attraction of Franklin Field for me was the quarter-mile cinder track, at the foot of a grassy hill, below the bowling green and a large stone and wood administration building known as the Head House because it was located at the head of the field that borders Blue Hill Avenue. It was on that track that I began to learn the exhilaration of excelling at something, to imagine every muscle I owned working to propel me faster and faster, to absorb these experiences, and to know at age twelve and thirteen that I was starting to feel like a man.

It was here that glory—even more, international fame—beckoned early and much too easily. And as I soon learned, such temptations of fame can be folly turned inside out. On one Fourth of July celebration, as Franklin Field swarmed with people, I was asked to run the mile against Gil Dodds. It didn't make sense, but an adult track official had asked, and I was not bold enough to refuse. Mr. Dodds was known as the Flying Parson because he was a minister, and because in indoor competitions, he had established the record as the fastest miler in the world. I was given a lead of at least a quarter of a mile on the champion, who prepared to start the run on the other side of the track. I had calculated a few things with certainty. I knew I could run a whole mile, but I also knew I couldn't survive the race if I tried to take my fifty-yard-dash speed and stretch it to 1,760 yards.

Shortly into the race, Mr. Dodds swept by. He may have swept by twice. I saw only the profile of the thin, bespectacled face and the legs and arms, which appeared to be two sets of tireless, bony pistons. Eventually I completed the mile, abandoned by the crowd and not displeased to cross the finish line unnoticed by the fans and autograph-seekers who surrounded the winner. Still, I took comfort from knowing that I had served a purpose. If I hadn't poked around the course, how would anyone have known how fast the Flying Parson had flown?

Another Fourth of July, I decided, would have to be different. Seventy-five or more boys—I don't recall seeing girls—showed up for the fifty-yard dash. The number of competitors was so cumbersome that officials gave up the idea of running a series of heats, which would eliminate the slower boys until an ultimate winner emerged. Instead, we were lined up across a section of grass adjacent to the cinder track. Track umpires bustled across the field, flustered and losing patience over the enormity of their task, attempting to line up seventy-five excited, knobby-kneed colts. I was somewhere in the middle of this herd, eager like the rest but curiously relaxed, prepared for my mission.

A white-shirted sleeve was raised, and the report of the starter's pistol resounded. I leaped from my crouch—no one could have rounded up seventy-five pairs of starting blocks—and ran, hearing nothing and staring at the line of red twine that had been stretched across the finish line, wanting with all my heart to bring it closer and closer. The blur of other boys to my left and right reached my brain. I dug harder and pulled ahead and then saw no one and ripped across the finish line, that sensation of twine bursting and fluttering on my chest bringing the sweetest feeling of my entire life.

The effort had taken only slightly more than six seconds. Running officials took me around the shoulders; youngsters and adults gathered around. A spoil sport speculated aloud that I looked older than thirteen. I was the winner of the Boston City Games, and I kept repeating that distinction to myself. The meet director handed me a small box. I have the contents now: a gold medal with a red, white and blue sash. It's in a frame on a shelf in my living room. It means more to me than the medals next to it, much harder wrought, that my wife Evelyn and I were given for completing the New York City Marathon.

On succeeding summers, after school was out and the track and field competitions were over, I returned to the cinder track at Franklin Field, convinced that I had the potential to be an Olympian. The field had given me promise as a sprinter, and the Fourth of July speeches from the balcony of the Head House had helped instill the beauty of the idea of representing America. Sometimes I coaxed other boys from the neighborhood to join me, but since I was the fastest and they had already attempted challenges and failed, they were usually not very interested.

One hot afternoon, as I did wind sprints around the track—a hundred yards at three-quarter speed, two-hundred yards at a fast jog, over and over again—a young woman materialized. She stood there, looking my way. Every two minutes or so I completed a lap and ran by her, noticing in an accumulation of images that her hair was brown, that she wore a white buttoned-up blouse, had on a gray-colored skirt and flat dark shoes. There was no one else around, and it became clear that she was there because of me. I was sixteen years old. She looked older. Finally my workout was over. We hadn't spoken, but I felt I couldn't just pack up my equipment bag and leave.

I approached her, and we looked at each other. She didn't smile, but she said, "Hi." I said "Hi" and felt nervous. I began to walk, and she walked with me. "You're a good runner," she said. "Thanks," I answered. We went up by the bowling green and along the paved walk in front of the Head House and out to Blue Hill Avenue, to where it intersects with Talbot Avenue. We crossed the street and went into a candy shop. She studied several glass cases and displays and made a choice. I bought her a bar of halvah, marble style.

We went outside. She unwrapped it, ate it slowly, looked at me one more time and walked back toward the intersection of Talbot Avenue and Blue Hill Avenue. All my training in Franklin Field had not prepared me for this. I didn't follow her. I didn't know what else to say. I didn't know what else to do. But I was filled with a strange excitement. I sensed, standing on the sidewalk, that there were going to be sweet new feelings, maybe even more memorable than breaking the twine and winning the race.

Heritage

The two experiences are represented by a set of hand cymbals. One experience unfolded in New England, the other a generation later in Westchester County, New York. The miniature brass cymbals have been etched by different hands and so appear on the surface to be distinctive. But strike them together and the sounds they make are identical.

We drove for an hour or two, my father and I, and when we finally pulled into the park grounds, the excitement was almost too much for a small boy to bear. Screeching fiddles, yelping children, exuberant drums, jabbering adults. The sounds all rose with the fragrant smoke of charcoal and lamb, creating a scene suggesting a joyous gypsy encampment. The scene was also a little frightening. There was anarchy, if jubilant anarchy, and only my father's assured behavior and the happiness on the faces of the darting youngsters kept me from bolting and racing back to our car.

It was what was then called a Syrian picnic, and it would take place once or twice a summer, organized by an Eastern Christian church but welcoming any Christian, Muslim, Jew or infidel who wanted to come and savor for an afternoon an abundant helping of Middle Eastern hospitality. If my mother, sister and brother were with us, the fact escapes my memory. Perhaps the captivation of the picnic and my father's hand were all my young mind could handle.

We returned to the picnic grounds as often as we could, but every Sunday at ten in the morning we also gathered around the radio for *The Arabic Hour*. It was the second component of my heritage training. Once again, my father's delight at hearing the music and the language shone in his eyes and the smiles that lit his face. But one day, after he had not taken me to a Syrian picnic for a long time, I asked him why. Being Jewish had been a most incidental detail in our trips. No longer. Things had changed, he said. We were still welcome, but he felt events on the other side of the world compelled him to stay away. "At the picnic, they're all gentiles," he said. He sounded miserable. I weighed it against the memory of his joy upon arriving at the picnic. I will spend the rest of my life weighing that moment.

My son Edward Salim was five years old, and it was time for him to learn about his heritage. I had been drilling him off and on for a year to count in Arabic and to say thank you and you're welcome. Shortly before, I had been the beneficiary of a wonderful instructor in Arabic at the Westchester Community College. Edward's "Syrian picnic" turned out to be a Middle Eastern restaurant run by a gentle and patient man known as Suleiman. He reminded me of my father when I was very young. Suleiman's experience with his restaurant was itself a lesson in being true to thyself.

He opened his doors to the hostility or indifference of many local people in Tarrytown, a Hudson River village, then tried to ingratiate himself and save his business by offering ham-and-egg breakfasts and white-bread lunches. The tactic failed, and he returned to service the fine Arabic foods he originally had intended. The restaurant hobbled along, supported by a handful of loyal customers and an enthusiastic band of county Arabs who would descend on weekend evenings. Two laudatory reviews swept in new and continuing patronage. Today, Suleiman seems happy, if not overwhelmed, by his success.

I brought Edward Salim, along with his mother, younger brother, and baby sister, to the restaurant. "Is this a special occasion?" Edward asked as we entered. He knew it was and faced it with all the delight but none of the fear his father ever knew. Edward and the other children were surprisingly fond of the food placed before them: whipped salads of mashed eggplant and chick peas mixed with sesame paste, sprightly seasoned green beans, broiled chopped lamb rolled with bulgur, pilaf, round loaves of fluffy bread.

The owner and his waiter, a tall, handsome Lebanese, made several trips to the table to hover and take pleasure as the food disappeared. In the background from a tape recorder came the perpetual screeching instruments and throaty groans of popular Arabic music. The sounds dissipated in the cotton rugs hung on the walls depicting dancing girls and desert oases.

Suleiman returned to ask if his dishes were enjoyed. A Muslim, he conveyed a tender persistence that there will be peace with Jews in the Old World. He was told that the evening was a special occasion for Edward, that we all prayed for peace, that the food was extraordinary and that Edward had something to say to him. I coached my son in a whisper.

"Shuk-ran," Edward said shyly.

"Ah, shuk-ran, shuk-ran [thank you]," said Suleiman. "Af-wan!"

Edward knew that meant "you're welcome."

Suleiman seemed to be enjoying the moment as much as my father did, wading in among the celebrants at the Syrian picnic. "Edward can do something else," I said. "He can count."

The waiter joined Suleiman. Both were intent on hearing every syllable. Edward, with only a trace of self-consciousness, began. "Wa-hed, ith-nain, tha-la-thah, ahr-baah, khoum-sah ..."

Suleiman was beside himself with pleasure. The waiter applauded. The daddy was proud to the point of tears. It was the kind of reception I had dearly hoped Edward would receive. Suleiman continued the count to ten. Edward echoed the numbers, though haltingly. Suleiman, wanting to stretch the joy of the moment, continued to fifteen. I nodded that Edward had already reached his academic summit. Suleiman understood, and the visit ended with profuse thanks and praise and promises of reunions.

Edward Salim, whose moods are normally reflected by wry and subtle tugs at the edge of the mouth or the lift of an eyebrow, beamed this night. Welcome, Edward. Join your father and his father. Welcome to the pride, the beauty, the bewilderment that is your heritage.

On Defining Family (September 11, 2001)

Let me start by telling you about what might be the last blissfully carefree day I'll ever have. It was Sunday, September 9, 2001. I sat in Yankee Stadium's right centerfield bleachers with my sons, Edward Salim and Charles Aram, and their college friend Marc from Providence. The Yankees played with aplomb; the Red Sox struggled. It was Marc's first visit to the great stadium, and he looked worried. "I don't expect the Sox to win," he said. "I just hope they don't lose by too much." We ate buns I'd brought from Chinatown, drank Cokes and bottled water. The late-summer sun baked us red and brown. Three burly young Sox fans who had driven down from Maine sat behind us. They became friendly in a reticent New England kind of way and asked for our ticket stubs as souvenirs. Charles and Marc left after eight innings. "I want to stay," Edward said. "I like it at the end when Frank Sinatra sings 'New York, New York.'" The final score was 8–2.

I thanked Edward for the ticket, and we kissed good-bye on the subway, which took me to Grand Central and the train home. Gazing lazily at the Hudson River as the train traveled north, I relished thoughts of how much our boys loved living and working in their city. My wife, Evelyn, drove me home from the station. Pleasure lit her face as I described the afternoon and the happiness of our sons. We read the papers, dined, watched the television news, and slept well.

Emerging from the Brooklyn Bridge–City Hall station just before 9:00 AM on Tuesday, September 11, from the same No. 4 subway that had taken us to Yankee Stadium, I joined a large pocket of people, many of whom I knew, staring up at the Twin Towers of the World Trade Center, five blocks south of my office. Billows of gray smoke, filled with sheets of paper floating like large confetti, blew east toward Brooklyn from one of the towers. "A small plane must have hit the building," someone said. "Maybe the pilot got lost or had a heart attack." It was a manageable thought. It was what we wanted to believe.

I waited in line to buy my usual coffee from the Russian husband and wife in the yellow wagon and turned back to look up. An enormous orange-red fireball suddenly erupted from the second tower. It took a moment to comprehend that it was real. The blast's horrible tongue seemed to lick the sky in slow motion, and it began to spit smoke and thousands of pieces of paper. A booming roar split the air. I didn't want to believe what I was seeing. "No!" I hollered. "Terrorists!"

The brick plaza shook. "Oh, my God!" people screamed. "I don't believe it!" Someone said it looked like a scene from a Hollywood movie. People began to run. Some stood petrified. The hundreds of pigeons that usually occupy the plaza were already gone. Three years ago, terrorists had bombed two American embassies in East Africa in quick succession. But this was an attack in downtown Manhattan. I feared there could be more. Harry, my coworker, came rushing up. His face was bright red, his eyes wet, his arms trembling. Harry is a career law-enforcement man, a member of an antiterrorism team, known for his cool and incisive manner. He had been standing even closer to the World Trade Center. He confirmed what I could not bring myself to utter. "They were jumping. People were falling from seventy stories up," he cried.

I waved my credentials and raced inside my building. I work as a press officer for the U.S. Attorney's Office, an arm of the Department of Justice. My office had prosecuted the men responsible for the 1993 World Trade Center bombing, which took six lives and injured more than a thousand people. And it had prosecuted two dozen defendants for other terrorist crimes linked to the Middle East, most recently the 1998 attacks on the U.S. embassies in Nairobi, Kenya, and Dar es Salaam, Tanzania, which left 224 dead. We also had indicted their purported leader, Osama bin Laden. "I'll hang in," I told the boss. "Go home," she said. I knew it sounded brash, but I tried again: "I'll hang in." She seemed neither pleased nor annoyed. "Go home," she said.

I called Evelyn to say I was unharmed and asked her to reach our sons in Manhattan and Sara Jameela, in Syracuse. Security officers were evacuating our nine-story building. I joined one of them. "Get out. Everyone is ordered out!" I shouted, then got out myself. On the building's front steps, fellow employees stared up at the staggering, nightmarish sight. Behind the blazing 110-story towers, the sky was an iridescent blue. And the air was charged with fearful expectation. I was standing in the middle of a cluster of government buildings, including the courthouse where terrorists had been tried, the jail where they were kept, and the headquarters of the FBI, which had captured them. My thoughts now were not to serve but to survive for my family and myself. (We soon learned from storefront TV sets and blaring radios in parked trucks that a plane had struck the Pentagon, near Washington, D.C., and another had plunged into the Pennsylvania countryside.)

One of the people next to me on the steps was Janice, also part of our antiterrorism unit. She commuted to work from out of state and didn't know the city. "I have to get to the Port Authority," she said. "I have to get a bus home." In the few moments I'd spent inside the building, I'd learned that all the tunnels and bridges were sealed and told her so. "Come with me," I said. "I'm going to start walking. I don't think going into the subway is safe. We'll do the best we can."

In that instant, we became sister and brother, refugees in our own homeland. Heartbroken, we joined the thousands of grim people streaming north, many covered with ash. Some were numb and silent; some wanted to tell anyone where they had been and what they had seen. Several wanted to pray. Many hugged. Others sat down in the gutter and held their head in their hands. Sirens wailed everywhere. It didn't look like America. It looked like a newsreel on war-torn Europe or Asia. But there was no baritone voice-over letting you know that you were safe in a movie house, that this was happening to somebody else. "Janice, let's just get out of this and get safe," I told her. "We can do our crying tonight."

On Sixth Avenue in Greenwich Village, hundreds of people began to shriek, "Oh, no!" I spun around to see several cars and trucks suddenly stop. Someone's been hit, I thought. But everyone was staring up. The second Twin Tower began to float down, floor by floor. It folded like a gigantic deck of cards, like it was not a building at all, but the finale of a grotesque magic act. It disappeared from the skyline, replaced by billowing clouds of smoke. Maneuvering through the warren of little streets in Soho and the Village, we had not realized the first tower was already gone, was already dust. We joined an orderly line at a pay phone and made calls. Janice learned she could stay with a cousin on the West Side. She was hungry, and we found a restaurant in the Garment Center whose name on this day swelled with significance. At the New Jerusalem, Janice ate kosher pizza while I sipped coffee.

Manhattan was an island filled with millions of agitated and grief-stricken people. Astonishingly, one of them closest to me walked through the restaurant door. James is another coworker, who, when we discovered how alike our values and sense of humor were, had become as close as a brother. We hugged. He introduced two women he'd run into. They were fleeing the United Nations and wanted his company and strength. My son Edward left his job at a securities firm and joined us. He wanted to protect me, and I welcomed the protection. He offered his apartment to any in our group trapped in town. Evelyn waited at Grand Central, from which she and I planned to try to escape the city. In the midst of this monstrous catastrophe, people were giving and receiving comfort, even momentary joy, surrounded by their families-real, extended, and accidental.

The night and days that followed brought many calls—my brother, Alvin, in California; Evelyn's brother, John, in upstate New York; writing students; an editor; the local cab dispatcher; someone I'd dated briefly almost thirty years ago. Everyone asked the exact same question: "Are you okay?" By then, we knew that Arab suicide terrorists had carried out the attacks with hijacked planes, that a worldwide manhunt was on for their leaders and accomplices. Like everyone, I fell into mourning for the people lost. I searched my thoughts for why this had happened. I experienced anger, rage, sorrow, feelings of helplessness. Nightmares came easily; ordinary sleep did not. I imagined the falling bodies, the defenseless victims on the planes, the bewilderment and shock of their families. I was uplifted by revelations of the courage shown by the passengers on the plane that fell in Pennsylvania. I also felt something I had never felt before. I am an Arab and a Jew, and have tolerated a lifetime of curiosity, affection, and even ridicule for being so. But as an Arab American, I had never before felt shame. Now, I felt the terrorists had disgraced me and every Arab—Muslim, Christian, and Jewish—everywhere on earth. I was still an Arab, but the terrorists had robbed me of my pride in saying so.

Evelyn fretted that our children might become victims of anti-Arab bias. "Hadad" is a quintessential Arab name, though it is more often spelled "Haddad." The so-called mastermind of the earlier bombing of the World Trade Center, Ramzi Yousef, had used eleven aliases. One of them was "Naji Haddad." We ran into a woman we've known for years. She snubbed us. Evelyn and I drove to a Red Cross center and a local hospital to donate blood. The center had a waiting period of more than five hours; the hospital said it would call us. The World Trade Center site was overrun with volunteers. Everyone wanted to try to understand the calamity, to ease their pain by participating in some way. The crime rate fell to zero.

We went to Evelyn's church. The church is a mile away from my Prayer Tree, in the hills of the Rockefeller family estate. After the suspected embassy bombers had been arraigned in New York, I'd gone to the tree to pray that the government had seized the people truly responsible. It seemed a long and innocent time ago.

Now, people were looking over their shoulder, feeling jittery, wondering what might happen next. I was desperate for a normalcy I knew deep down might not be attainable. I shopped for fresh groceries, changed bed linens, bought new garbage pails, scrubbed sinks. It was a ritual cleansing of the home, as if that might wash away the indelible memories.

Our son Charles, a news producer, called: "I'm on the street. CNN has been evacuated. Is it on TV?" Evelyn and I wondered how long it might be before he would love his city freely again. He soon let us know. A few nights later, at 2:00 AM, Charles carried an amplifier to his open fourth-story window on Manhattan's East Side, plugged in his guitar, and played an inspired rendition of "The Star Spangled Banner." Not a cop in New York would have filed a complaint. The same night, his brother Edward, happening into the gloom of a tavern near Madison Square Garden, began to sing the same anthem, filling the room, at least for the moment, with pleasure and hope. "You knew all the words?" I asked the next day. "I hummed some," he said.

I'd met Robert Windrem, an investigative producer at NBC News, at a terrorist trial. We'd grown to like each other. He called to say his teenage son had asked him why the Twin Towers were destroyed. "Few people in this country know more about terrorism than me," he told his son. "But that still doesn't help me understand it."

Almost 350 firefighters perished following the attack. Danny Kane of Woodside, Queens, is a retired, decorated New York City firefighter who later worked with his son Daniel as an ironworker. Danny is another of my brothers in spirit. "This is a condolence call," I said over the phone. "We've been down there for three days," he said of the World Trade Center site. "Essentially, we're taking big pieces of metal and making them small enough to haul away on trucks. It's a place I never want to see again." I asked why, after days of failure, they continued to search the rubble for survivors. "The firefighters had no intention of fighting the fire. They went in to rescue people and save lives," Danny said. "Everyone knows in their heart no one's left alive, but no one wants to admit it."

A letter arrived from Steven Selman, a friend since high school, a fellow Northeastern University graduate and a retired Army colonel: "I thought it might help if I sent you this note of support in light of the horrible events of the last days. It must not be easy to be a Hadad living and working so close to what used to be the WTC. Hang in there." I returned to my office, a place where people are mostly kind and friendly and very smart. Its conviction rate is over 95 percent. Upon seeing each other, some colleagues wept. Many kissed or embraced. One said he was through mourning; he was angry, and he wanted to get the bastards. That became the universal word on the street to describe the hijackers and their accomplices. I ran into Harry, who had witnessed the falling bodies and who once told me his retirement dream was running a hotdog stand at the beach. "I'm sorry you had to see what you did," I said in private. "I've thought a lot about you." "I'm okay," he replied.

It had been seven days since the attack. Smoke continued to rise from where the skyscrapers once stood. The air was foul. A press office colleague and I secured breathing masks and headed downtown. Cops, state troopers, and National Guardsmen maintained posts on every corner. The streets were crowded. People took snapshots. We got as far as the corner of Nassau and Liberty streets, two small blocks from the center of the disaster. The view was mesmerizing. The rising smoke suggested purgatory. It stung your eyes, scratched your throat. Huge sheaths of twisted metal remained vertical, as if hurled with great force into the ground from above. They were the remains of the lower floors. "I've seen enough," I told my coworker. "I know a way back where the smoke won't be as bad." We zigzagged back through old and cramped streets and came upon something we hadn't expected. It was a narrow building with a small canopy and a sign that read "Wall St. Synagogue." Such a modest edifice for such an imposing name. Two cops, one a lieutenant, were coming out. We began to reach for our credentials when the lieutenant said, "No, just go in. We were praying, too." My companion said, "They looked more Irish than Jewish." I knew he was right.

In the small sanctuary, I put my mask on top of my head as a yarmulke, and we sat down in a pew near the pulpit in the center of the room. I thanked God for protecting my family. I told Him of my despair over the loss of the thousands of lives in the World Trade Center and the Pentagon, on the four planes. It was the eve of Rosh Hashanah, and I asked for a different kind of New Year, one filled with peace. We emerged back onto the street. Squeezed next door to the temple was a firehouse wide enough for only one truck. A firefighter stood in the doorway. I wanted desperately to talk to him but couldn't find the words. I couldn't say, "Are you okay?" Five firefighters from Engine Company 6 had sped to the Twin Towers. He was the only one who'd come back.

A few hours later, my day's work was done, and Evelyn and I relished a diversion from the week's events—the comfort of a brief reunion with close Boston friends. Lise and Myles Striar were in New York to see their daughter Maria perform in an Off-Broadway play. They joined us at a sidewalk café on Park Avenue near Grand Central. It was a beautiful early evening. Passersby seemed calm, or as calm as New Yorkers ever look as they dash to their next appointment. There was a blessed absence of cell phones, and Myles marveled that there was almost no horn honking. The drinks were excellent. We toasted each other and our good fortune to be together and remembered those lost in the attacks. The sun was setting. A bracing hint of chill was folded into the air. We got comfortable, the conversation became more animated, and we decided to stay together for one more.

Myles caught me paying unusual attention to the sidewalk traffic. "What are you doing?" he asked. "I'm trying to determine who are more stunning, the women walking south or the women walking north," I said. He joined in with me. Relaxing at a café with three people I love, watching the girls go by, felt good. It felt frivolous. It felt defiant. I was a New Yorker, and I wanted my city back. I was an American, and I wanted my country back. I needed to believe that the future would once again hold for all of us a blissfully carefree day.

Monogamy Mon Amour

We were swapping male small talk over martinis and spicy rice crackers when my friend said knowingly, "The first time's always the hardest." His remark begged a reply but I was caught in a turmoil of emotions: envy of his experience, indignation that he cheated on his wife, pleasurable anticipation of what more he might reveal, shame that I had nothing to contribute.

I masked my feelings with silence and a smile, and the conversation moved on to jobs, children, and the lunch menu, but my thoughts remained riveted on the earlier topic. How often does he meet other women, where does he meet them, what does he say? What if they ask if he's married, or suggest he get lost, or pour a drink over his head, or say "yes?" I found I was working hard to convince myself of my higher moral standing, but I had to be honest.

How could I equate righteousness with my curiosity about women other than my wife? Despite my deeply felt love and devotion to her over many years, how did I explain my flirtatious manner at the office; my exploring of pretty faces on the street; my intense, if romantic, belief that I was a one-man sexual National Guard, in perpetual preparedness for infidelity.

A surprise call came recently from a woman in New England. It was terrible news. She said my longtime friend, the man who'd taught me about the woods and hiking and climbing up mountains, was dead. Cancer. She said she had been his mistress twenty years ago and that they had a daughter. She said my friend had married her two weeks ago (she was his third wife) and asked that I be told he was dying. "I know you," she added. "You used to visit his old house when I was the babysitter." I felt grief for my friend but curiosity about this woman. I discussed her call with my wife, and we decided to invite my friend's new wife and their daughter to visit.

They came. The woman described holding my friend in her arms as he died and how happy she was finally to carry his name. Our eyes were moist many times over the three days, but she was cheerful and resilient. By the time we waved good-bye to our new friends, Evelyn and I learned they had left us—in addition to the wine and the basket of good country fruits and sausage—with feelings unexamined and, until now, unspoken.

While our children played outside, my wife and I poured coffee and began talking in the kitchen, which faces the woods and where most of our important talking gets done. My wife talked about how the woman had gone from bride to widow in two weeks and how she deserved a better life in all those years my friend had been married to someone else. And then my wife's natural grace expanded and she astonished me. "I'd permit you one affair," she said. Her frankness prompted me to blurt out, "You're certainly more generous than I think I could be." "If you kept going out with other women I think I'd leave," she said. "But one fling, I think I could understand that."

We had on occasion discussed monogamy, she feeling it is part of the natural order, I arguing it is a socially imposed necessity but easy to conform to, especially with a lovely and responsive wife like her. Also, I had once read that marriage is the only adventure open to the cowardly, and I had taken that as a challenge. I compared extramarital affairs to prizefighting because both involve taking large chances. While I'd had no real experience in the former, I'd had a few prizefights as a very young man. "They used to say," I'd told her, "that when you start to think about getting hurt, it was time to stop stepping in to the ring." How little I knew then that my big shot at a main event was about to occur.

At a business party I ran into a woman I knew slightly, who said a woman I used to know better had asked about me, and a short time later the woman I knew better telephoned and said we had to meet. I had in fact liked her very much and she had remained among the top names in my mythical roster of incomplete passes.

I invited her to lunch. We ate and talked and parted. She called again. We ate and talked and kissed, tentatively, on the street and parted. She called a third time, obviously sick of eating. She said she had put together a master plan, complete with alibi, for keeping me in town for the night and consummating those lunches. Flattery suddenly turned into flabbergast. I was breathless. Then I began to back-pedal furiously. She tried to convince me of the beauty of the idea, then rather good-naturedly gave up. I succumbed that day to telling the story to a man who knew us both. He was impressed, which was the petty idea. "But she called my bluff, and I chickened out," I said. Maybe I was a coward, but it didn't feel that bad.

In the kitchen that evening, the older two children at homework in other parts of the house, a TV droning, the cat nodding on our best couch, the old stereo piping in Mozart, I poured two glasses of wine, handed one to my wife and raised my own: "To the ultimate fling," I said. My wife was silent, and I saw in her usually guileless blue eyes doubt and skepticism. After several moments she smiled and pushed her glass toward mine, and the clink was a beautiful, one-note song. It was so good to be home.

Fantastic Journey

I made an extraordinary discovery at the age of twelve. By merely touching my thumb to forefinger and pressing, I could disrobe women. If I pressed gently, only their outer clothing disappeared. If I pressed really hard, everything flew off. I never tried it on men—what in the world for?—and it never occurred to me to try it on children. Oh, what a wholesome pervert I was. But my discovery was magic on grown-up women, which was any girl over fifteen, and it worked especially well on beautiful women.

I usually practiced this skill from the protection of the bus on the way to school. I shuddered to think what might happen if a woman detected what I was up to. "I caught this young scoundrel pressing his thumb to his forefinger!" she might have shouted, holding me by the ear as the crowd gathered and the police raced to the scene. I could not have survived the condemnation. How would I have explained it to my mother and older sister? (I never looked at either one of them. I swear it.) What would the teachers and the principal have done to me at school?

Still, I liked to believe I didn't abuse this power. In more than a few instances, sensing that a particular subject did not approve of being naked to my glance on the street corner, I quickly pulled my fingers apart. But it was all the beginning of a lifetime of fascination, homage, folly, devotion, absurdity, anguish, ineptitude, infatuation, despair, adoration, and love—to name some of the conditions—I've experienced with women.

As I grew older I put my magical skill aside (within reach as needed and periodically called upon) for more subtle forms of appreciation.

In the next few decades, I learned many things. I learned, for instance, that one didn't have to lunge at a woman with desperate, hopeless abandon to achieve physical contact. Women enjoyed humor and many other forms of intellectual stimulation and rewarded them. They loved swapping opinions, finding out things they didn't know, and teaching things they did. They enjoyed being hard-nosed with men; they enjoyed being sentimental. They appreciated loyalty, they loathed servility, they sometimes encouraged intrigue.

With this vast knowledge and a great deal of luck, I married a wonderful woman and became a father three times. All of which placed me, as an equal-opportunity husband, in the supermarket one recent afternoon. The stranger's shopping cart and mine arrived at the same place at the same time. She and I also were looking for the same item, an antidote for indigestion. I reached for the brand-name product and then spotted the store's knock-off.

"Have you ever tried it?" I asked. "No, let's see if it has the same ingredients," she said. We studied labels. I bumbled through "Active Ingredient: Bismuth Subsalicylate" on the $1.99 product. She did the same on the $3.49 bottle.

"I'm trying the cheaper one," I said. "Me, too," she said. "Now we can afford to get heartburn more often," I said. She thought that was pretty funny. As she threw her head back and laughed, I noticed she looked at me closely, up and down. Then our carts moved on.

The episode left me feeling discernibly good. My spirits rose. I even skipped a little behind my shopping cart. What a curious, pleasant, civil give-and-take it had been, I thought. She wasn't beautiful. She had a nice sense of humor. Maybe she was really a blonde. She had an easy, unforced self-confidence. She looked all right in jeans, but nothing more. Her laugh was musical. Undoubtedly she, like I, was shopping for her family.

I saw her again in canned tuna, decided she was quite alluring, and kept moving. If my long and picaresque career with women had taught me anything it was this: Never try to recapture a moment on a sea beach at sunrise; in a steamy, rhythm-driven barroom; or in the aisle at the Pepto-Bismol shelf.

Down by the cat food, it hit me. I could almost feel the heel of the hand bouncing off my forehead. I suddenly knew exactly why I felt so terrific. The woman had just undressed me! I knew it. I felt it. Maybe laughing was her magic. During the few minutes it had taken us to settle the heartburn remedy question, she had sized me up as her fantasy. I had become her sex symbol. I can't tell you rationally why that was so important, but for a few euphoric moments, I was preposterously, senselessly happy.

Fidelity

My mother and father are the guests of my wife and me in an ornate restaurant. We want the experience to be special because they have been married for fifty years. They are agitated, however, by the prices on the menu. They tell the waiter who rolls the pastry cart over that for the cost of the slender pieces of cake he is offering they expect to take the rest of the cake home.

The wine is delicious. My mother raises her glass, looks at my father with a smile and says, "To the only man I ever slept with." My father's eyes are twinkling, and he is smiling back at my mother. His look reveals amusement, nothing more. I turn to look at my mother, with admiration. With one simple statement she has said enough to fill a book: about her fidelity, about her sense of mischief, about my father's infidelity. It is an accusation, it is a truce, it is an anniversary revelation that she knows all, an admission that she knows nothing, an assurance that there is nothing to know.

It is Saint Valentine's Day, forty years ago. I am on my hands and knees under the old kerosene stove on the linoleum floor, sniffling and bawling, picking up chocolates and their brown paper cups and trying to fit them back into the heart-shaped box. Behind me, my father, the giver of the candy, stares at my mother, the flinger of same. She is furious and hot; he is sullen and cold. My baby brother watches from his high chair.

I collect about two-thirds of the box. I will be the great conciliator. I stop crying long enough to proffer the candy to my mother. She refuses and nods me away. Even my pitiful state has failed to melt her or my father. I return to safety under the stove and comfort myself by sampling the chocolates.

My wife and I join my older sister and her husband for dinner, shortly after the big anniversary. We are discussing my parents, particularly my mother's complex and mercurial personality and how it plays against my father's seeming serenity, which on occasion has been interpreted as cowardice.

Our mood is upbeat. I suggest that my mother would have been a brilliant vaudevillian. She could turn our family hysterical with laughter doing her wicked imitation of my Egyptian aunt, hissing and gargling in a parody of the spoken Arabic. My mother could also toss back her head and belt out "One of These Days" with so much power and bathos that the great Sophie Tucker, happening by, might have taken a seat and listened to how it ought to be done. Or she could reduce you to warm, melancholy tears when she whispered the words, "In my sweet little Alice blue gown …"

As they say of all great clowns, my mother yearned to be taken seriously, tragically, and since crying seems more serious than laughing, that song became her favorite.

My father, I tell the group at table, is much harder to characterize. He is a man of quiet, almost hidden, elegance. My father's old business cards read, "Distributor of General Merchandise." He was a peddler with a sense of class. He might have made a great, older screen lover, say a Charles Boyer, without all that Gallic salad dressing, or a masterful clergyman, the kind that late in life humbly announces that he thinks he might have an acceptable explanation for an elusive Talmudic riddle. He is popular with the old women of his community; he is a groundbreaker, a leader in the temple. How does one reconcile movie idol and rabbi, I am asked. I see no contradiction. Both practice seduction, I say, but only one is after your soul.

Suddenly, in the midst of this pleasurable if giddy small talk, my sister hurls a lightning bolt: Daddy had an affair while Mother was in the hospital giving birth to our brother. It was with Mother's sister. The statement affects me as if I were blinded. I flail and demand details and proof. My sister elaborates, riding the emotion of her own declaration, and soon the matter is at least partially clear. She is repeating a tale apparently learned at our mother's elbow. She seems to have taken the bones of the story, turned it over many times in her head, added her own belief of male fickleness and is now presenting as fact her grown-up version of words heard as a young girl.

Just as suddenly as I was blinded, I decide the story is silly and demonstrate this by clapping and saying, "Well, good for him." Yet, there remains that possibility that my sister is not all wet; there is that slanting light entering the mind, a picture illuminated through Venetian blinds and therefore distorted, of that long-gone but unforgettable Saint Valentine's Day in the kitchen. My sister must see doubt crossing my face, for she blurts out, "He did it, and I have never forgiven him!"

It is four years since my parents' fiftieth wedding anniversary, and the bickering between them has increased. My mother does not sing much or dance anymore, on the dubious grounds that her son-in-law does not approve. But she can still tell a good story, and when she laughs the sound thrills me. My discreet and patient father has taken to open complaint and confrontation with her. They argue not so much about health as about worries about health. They argue over the qualities of the neighbors, the shortcomings of their children, whether the water is sufficiently hot for tea. It makes me wonder if marriages last a lifetime or if they wear out, like everything else.

My father sends me a letter. It reads:

Your Mother and I are not getting along. She would like to stay with Katie [my mother-in-law in New York City, 200 miles from their home in Boston] for a while. She is impossible to live with.

Love, Dad.

P.S.: She will pay her own way.

I fret over the letter. Though the arrangement is unworkable, the request for it seems to show the chasm that has opened up between them. The letter reminds me of an earlier, troubling conversation I had with my father. I had asked that he and my mother relocate to be close to my family, which includes three children they adore. "Later," my father had replied, "after your mother …"

Two weeks pass. I telephone, prepared to say the Katie arrangement has been weighed and rejected, expecting to find two cold and unhappy voices on the line. My father, I learn, is experiencing dizziness upon lying down at night and getting up, and neurological tests have been inconclusive. He relates the condition without emotion. My mother takes the phone, and her concern is passionate. In her old woman's voice, the aggravation and hopelessness is replaced with a strength that almost causes me to pull the phone away from my ear. "I never loved a man like I love your father!" she says. The subject of Katie never comes up.

The telephone call finds me at an office. My mother is in the hospital, she has been unconscious, it is very serious. I gather up my family and speed to Boston. Outside her room, a young doctor fills me in and tries to assure me she is past the threat of losing her life. But there is more bad news. After they got her to the hospital and revived her, they gave her a checkup. The doctor dances around the word "cancer" until I utter it. They think they can treat her successfully, he says, but urges me to help place her in a nursing home.

He says that is also the strong opinion of the doctor in charge of the case, and at his suggestion, the hospital has already made contact with the home where she should be sent. I reach the doctor in charge by phone the next day. He tells me it's "inconvenient" to meet but that it is imperative my mother be placed in the nursing home. I tell every word to my father. My sister, who lives nearby, supports the wisdom of the doctor. I am tempted to agree. She will get the kind of care she needs, and my father will then have the peace of mind and measure of freedom he seems to need. It is a neat solution. It makes sense.

I have no intention, however, of keeping any of these discussions and plans from my mother. Painstakingly, I repeat my conversation with the chief doctor and why he feels it is a good idea for her to try the nursing home. She recognizes the name of the home. Even in her misery, she is able to make me laugh. "I couldn't go there," she says, matter-of-factly. "That place is for nuts."

I return my family to our home and telephone my mother daily at the hospital. Sometimes my father is there. When he isn't, I call until I reach him at home. I feel an obligation to stay in constant touch until the move is complete.

The morning my mother is to leave the hospital, I reach my father. In a few minutes, he tells me, he will be leaving for the hospital. I ask if everything is set at the nursing home. His answer stuns me and makes me feel ashamed. "I'm not doing it, dear. She wouldn't be happy. I'm bringing her home," he says.

Is this habit, loyalty, fear of loneliness, religious conviction, love? All of these, probably. Is it fidelity? Yes. Oh, yes.

Brothers

I hadn't seen my brother in almost five years. He came on a Friday night and was gone back to California by Sunday afternoon. We got to talk alone twice, once while I did the Saturday grocery shopping, picked up wine, looked at a table, and checked out a rug sale, and again on Sunday just before he had to go.

Sunday's talk seemed far more significant, because Saturday's had to be given over partly to clearing the cobwebs and reducing the protective pretense to a minimum. Then again, Sunday's talk—held over a groaning board representing every cuisine from Hong Kong to Aleppo, from the Via Appia to Main Street—was propelled by alcohol. Alvin, always an experimenter, tested the Rob Roys. I defended the Scotch against its moral enemy, water.

Statements that reeked of profundity the moment they were uttered were all but lost by nightfall, when I prayed for his safe flight. Miracle of the mind, by Monday morning the important words returned, and I began to try putting them in some perspective, knowing it would be the best information available until the next time, no matter how many telephone calls or notes came in between.

Alvin is the same age as Jack Benny always was, only for real. He is working for a big telecommunications company, making his way, paying his bills, walking tall. In his spare time, he delves into some Eastern disciplines, which may be part Alvin and part California, but my brother has always been drawn to the Eastern part of the world for his private answers.

He has not always been on his feet financially, and it warmed my heart to see his pleasure, upon arriving, at dispensing lavish gifts to everyone in my household. My wife Evelyn and I received an L. L. Bean blanket; the boys, stylish winter jackets; our little daughter, a soft red-and-blue knit suit and beret.

My brother weighs fifteen or twenty pounds more than he should, and he is too vain about his still-abundant but falling hair. I don't talk from a perch of superiority. I am at least ten pounds beyond fighting weight and affect a crew cut from which a good deal of the crew has bailed out.

Alvin maintains a habit I once found annoying but now almost enjoy. He is fond of pontificating. At one point, he began to lecture me on child-rearing, with an eye toward avoiding spoiled children. I don't know why he stopped. I like to think it was because he has absolutely no experience, compared to my daily parental workout. But it might have been because he suddenly felt it was poor form for a guest.

My brother does know many things, and I was happy to learn some of them. He told me what woods make the best table, what constitutes a strong trestle, and what methods of fastening joint-to-joint are most trustworthy. He told me how to repair wallpaper that had been devastated by children's feet hanging off a banister, and he demonstrated the skill. At times, I found it amazing that we had come from the same house and had learned such vastly different things.

Alvin told me that he never expected to replace the friends he had in the Northeast with new ones on the West Coast. The East Coast produced deeper people, he felt, people with more staying power. The West Coast, for all its attractions, was inhabited by "air-heads." He said he might or might not ever marry and have children, though his affection for mine was instantaneous and unselfconscious. He worried about the material responsibility, among others. Yes, he was lonely from time to time, but I was not to worry about him as a result, for he filled most of his time as he wished. He refused casual liaisons with even the most pretty West Coast women because he felt such relationships were useless. He came to my home with a girlfriend of long standing from Boston. She was a friend, he explained, suggesting she always would be.

When my brother was very small and I was only slighter bigger, I bought him a pair of springs, the kind you tug across your chest until you look like Charles Atlas or some latter-day muscle man. I think Alvin would have developed just beautifully anyhow, but he credits the springs and so is unendingly grateful to me. What was less gratifying was the feeling that as I made my way in life my brother felt hopelessly outdistanced, and so for a while he withdrew from the race. He continued to read and take college courses and maintain friendships, but he stopped striving in the workaday world, and I felt at least partly responsible. As a result, I had never mentioned salaries and downplayed promotions and other achievements.

But in our conversation at my home, he talked openly about his earnings and how he hoped to increase them with a promotion within his company very soon. His talk had the effect of lifting the curse of living in the dust of the older brother. He wanted to know how much we had paid for the house he was seeing for the first time. It was more than either my brother or I could really afford.

"Nothing doing, Al," I said. "discretion dictates."

The fact was I loved him too much to let this dollar-sign shadow fall over him—over both of us—now. The son of a gun persisted and finally took a stab at the price. I don't think I have to worry about my brother Alvin anymore. He guessed almost right on the button.

Tennis

I have become a tennis widower. I know I still have a wife because she continues to take pains to raise our children at home properly and tend to my creature comforts. I even see her from time to time, most often freshening up playing togs, re-taping the handles of her racquets, or packing a new tin of balls into her bag.

Every now and then, we even get to sit down for a late supper. Here is a recent conversation.

Me: "How's your schedule look over the next several days, dear?"

She: "Well, let's see. There's a doubles tomorrow morning at the Tarry Crest Club, and I have a game with a new woman I met at Pocantico, and, oh, I'm so glad you asked. I have a lesson Thursday evening; it's the overhead smash this week. And, of course, Friday morning, there's the regular mixed doubles group, and I think it's next Wednesday that we have that interclub tournament at Ardsley."

It all began innocently enough. Before we were married, I'd meet Evelyn near our apartments on Manhattan's West Side, we'd stroll to Riverside Park with our racquets, and spend an hour or so slapping the ball against a cement wall. Sometimes we'd amble over to a nearby cinder track to run for a mile or so until one day, with a lap to go, I said, "I'm pouring it on." She passed me fifty yards later as if I were sitting down. "Let's go back to the well," I suggested.

Almost twenty years, two homes, and three children later, the mistake of that moment on the cinder track returned to strike me like a serve that hits the clay and explodes up into your chest. No, that's not quite accurate. I can't say I didn't see it coming. It was more like a lob that sailed up, completed its arc, and came down on top of my head.

If I had to choose a date in history that began my trip to tennis widowerhood, I'd guess it was the time in the early 1970s when we watched Billie Jean King mop up the court with Bobby Riggs. I was amused by Evelyn's feminine enthusiasm. But the week we began our blissful adventure as newlyweds in a suburban bungalow, the evidence became clear. We'd play at the village courts, grab some time at the local college, get invited to the local club, then spend spare time watching the pros on television.

Strange thing is, I was helping to train her and didn't even know it. Not until very late in the game did I realize I was doing anything more than getting a workout myself. Come Christmas time, there was never a hint about jewelry or clothing. But a new racquet would be terrific. At birthdays, the most cherished gift became membership to an indoor tennis club.

Well, the week of the conversation that included the discussion of five tennis dates without pause for mention of turmoil in the Middle East, the state of public education, or grubs in the grass, I decided on a brilliant strategy. "Evelyn, I haven't played in a while," began the crocodile. "Why don't we go out Sunday and belt the ball around." I intended to put all this tennis mania in its proper perspective.

Fifty minutes after we stepped onto the court, the set and match were mercifully over. I had illustrated this perspective 3–6. It would have been 2–6 except the Almighty delivered to me two impossibly beautiful passing shots in the next-to-last game. As we walked off, my wife allowed as how I looked terrific, considering I hadn't played in a few years. She also let slip that, out of delicately balanced combination of love and dread, she'd taken it easy on me.

I'm not through. There remains ways to return equilibrium to our marriage, though I'm not sure I'm ready to take the steps. I could take up golf. But when I think about it, I'd rather stay home by myself. I hate golf.

Trees

The tulip tree was dead. Its long furled leaves, pointing skyward like the fingernails of an elegant woman, would never again green and open. The leaves merely clung to the twigs held by the branches that sprouted from the shaft of the trunk, all of them ossified last fall when lightning struck.

My family had kept a kind of vigil through the early spring, hoping and watching for signs of new life, even peering up through binoculars. More than once I had cozied up to the trunk, three or more feet in diameter, hoping to feel some life, taking comfort in the sight of its ninety-foot height.

But soon the tulip tree was surrounded by lush growth, rendering it even more dark and solemn in its bareness, and nature was not yet through with it.

One recent morning I looked out, and it seemed as though some agitator had rushed up and hurled paint against the trunk. I went out and got close and was repulsed at the touch of a fungus of coral-colored slime. Don't try to treat it, take the tree down, recommended the nurseryman. Just as sure as lightning found the tallest tree on your property, it might seek it out again, and a second time, he said, the weakened tree could take your house with it.

Spiritually, I was not unprepared for the bad news. I tried to think like the Indians who once inhabited the same land, tried to assume their belief that I did not really own the tulip tree or anything else but only had the privilege of enjoying it, giving care and receiving benefit. It was right, the Indians told me, to hope the tree might survive. It was wrong to be angry or sad because I might be losing something I really didn't possess.

The very same day I accepted death of the tulip tree and put it to the back of my mind, I became preoccupied with the new life of the spring garden—planting the tomatoes, parsley, and basil; putting in flats of my wife Evelyn's favorite zinnias; getting in sunflower seeds for pleasure of the children (and the nutrition of the birds); sprinkling in a few fancy seeds here and there, such as Chinese poppy and a golden English daisy. I even tried some hollyhock seeds because the long gangly flowers reminded me of the neighborhood where I was a small boy.

Taking a break during this activity, I wandered over to the edge of our unruly woodpile. I had pleasant memory of the spot because two autumns ago one of my boys had brought home from school a pocketful of chestnuts. We had scratched loose a patch of earth, put the nuts in, covered them, and watered the area for a few days. Nothing had appeared the next spring or summer, and the chestnuts were forgotten. The children and their friends must have trampled over the site a hundred times in the warm weather; I did so almost as often, hauling up wood during the winter.

But this day something was growing. I got closer; it was not a plant or weed I could recognize. I remembered the planting of the chestnuts. I contained myself, but the idea that they might have finally begun to sprout was startling and exciting. I ran back to the house and up the stairs to the bookcase, where after several minutes of rummaging, I located a pocket book on trees. In it there was a sketch of a mature chestnut tree and a close-up of the leaves. I ran with the booklet back down to the woodpile and held the picture next to the plants. The leaves seemed to match in shape as well as color. I counted, and there were eight separate plants.

Still, I was reluctant to accept my own conclusion. Maybe it was a coincidence that these six-inch growths looked like trees. There were certainly volumes that I didn't know about things growing. I located another book in the house, and it described the great role the chestnut once played in America, cultivated for lumber and beauty, as well as its terrible demise by blight. It talked of the pleasures of strolling down Parisian boulevards beneath grand chestnut boughs. I raced back to the woodpile with the second book and compared plants and pictures. They were chestnut trees!

I paused for a moment, enchanted by the fact that, in my own perception at least, the tulip tree died and the chestnut trees came alive on the same afternoon. I became filled with a sense of gratitude.

No one was home. I had to tell someone the wonderful news. I tried to think of people to telephone. No one came to mind. I went outside for another look and came back in. Suddenly I knew what I wanted to do.

I went down to the new chestnut trees and fashioned a little protective fence around them. Then I stood, looked into the sky and thanked the Indians.

On Being Shy

I have this theory about shy people. They can be wonderful friends but they never stop being shy. As a result they prefer their friends to live far away. That explains why some of my best friends are little more than pen pals. It also explains my son Charles's dream.

In the dream, Charles has accidentally broken some object and has been ordered by a scolding teacher to the superintendent's office. But his friend Stephen appears, and together they enter a secret passage that leads to the sea, where they don underwater equipment and swim to safety, which turns out to be the real-world small pond outside the school.

I was stirred by the story and it reminded me of an essay Charles wrote for class shortly before the dream titled, "My Best Friend." It went:

> Do you have a best friend? I do. His name is Stephen Kim. He used to be a Cub Scout. Stephen has black eyes and straight black hair. Stephen likes to wear striped shirts. He's about my size. I like being with Stephen because he's friendly and he cheers me up when I'm sad. I like Stephen because he likes to do the same things I do. He's great.

Undoubtedly, Stephen is great, except last year he and his family moved away to Michigan. It bothered me that my son, who was not yet nine years old, was having spells of sadness and feeling the need to be cheered up by a best friend so far away. I thought back, with lurking uneasiness, to my chronic bouts of shyness and the consequences— the jobs and friends and girls never won. I remembered my joy upon learning there might be an honorable place for me, the day the literature professor said, "A writer is a shy actor."

Even as a very small boy Charles's shyness became legend. When he tried out for soccer, he showed his discomfort with the rules of the game and the strangers all around him by keeping one hand nonchalantly in the pocket of his shorts. He ran down the field as fast as the next player and kicked at the ball recklessly, but all the while he maintained his reserve, hand in pocket, as the adults on the sidelines fell over with laughter.

He was obliged at one time to join his day-camp class in an outdoor concert. Hundreds of folding chairs were set up for the audience, and Charles filed out with the rest of the children and marched obediently to his position. But the moment the musical director raised his arm for the first sweet, raucous note, Charles spun around. I believe he sang, but he sang the entire concert facing a brick wall.

He and I are both the middle-born of three children, and that must account for something. There was, to be sure, celebration at our births but, compared with our siblings, maybe we were taken for granted, neglected. Maybe we knew we were expected to be good and endearing and not much trouble. Even as his father, I don't have the answer, but that would explain why Charles has done a lot of his thinking by himself, often arriving at novel conclusions. One memorable example:

It was a steamy spring afternoon, and Charles watched as I hosed down the side of our modest house, washing away the various leavings of nature. Concern suddenly altered his face. "What is it?" I asked. He broke the news gently. "That won't make the house grow, you know."

I began to be preoccupied by Charles's dream. He had revealed the dream only after coaxing and, with the "My Best Friend" essay, it set off an odd and powerful ambition. I wanted to join Charles and Stephen in the secret passage and take the long and pleasurable voyage with them to the sea. I wanted to protect my son from unfair accusations and scolding teachers and stern-faced superintendents. But I knew I had to wait for the right moment to make my request.

Several nights later Charles, playful and with a laugh capable of healing, entered the living room and asked me to dance. To a radio piano concerto, we took hold of each other and began to imitate a ballroom dance. He took particular delight in the way we thrust out our arms in the manner of a cabaret tango.

After a while I said, "Charles, may I ask you something? You know the secret passage that you and Stephen have? Do you think there might be room in there for me?"

He was quiet. Then he said, "I don't know." He sounded burdened, and I knew I did not belong in there.

We continued to hold each other and move around the living room. Charles looked into my eyes. "You're a great dancer, Dad," he told me.

Facts of Life

"Your son wants to speak to you," said my wife over the telephone. I was busy at an office, but I always enjoy a few minutes with him. Seeing him every day makes it hard to gauge his growing up, but hearing his voice on the phone is a pretty good way to detect change.

"Dad, you got some mail from *Playboy*. Is it okay to open it up?" Gone now was the baby voice, the endearing lisp, the pitch that disguises gender. At nine going on ten, he sounded articulate and self-assured.

"What's it look like, Edward? Maybe we ought to wait 'til I get home."

He described the envelope, saying it seemed to be advertising some kind of contest. I used that information to stall him. "Better leave it alone, dear. I always enter those contests, you know, one day we might win a million. College for you and your brother and sister. Mink coat for Mom. And her law school tuition. The beach house for your old man."

That night, he and the mail were waiting for me at the door. The envelope was plastered with miniature Playboy covers, the photographs of the models just big enough to tantalize you into looking inside. I let him open it. The material included an inducement to take out a subscription and an offer to enter a contest for various prizes. There were no larger photographs of Playboy girls, and I saw the disappointment on my boy's face.

"There's a lesson in all this, Edward, it has to do with judging books by their covers. Or letters by their envelopes. Or, for that matter, women by what they may or may not be wearing."

It became clear in mid-sentence that I didn't know what I was talking about, and he interrupted me.

"Dad, when can we go to Grand Central Terminal again?"

This seemed a strange reaction, even though the children and I love riding the railroad. Then I caught on. "Are you interested in the famous ceiling of the grand concourse, or the exquisite carving at the platform entrances, or perhaps the large number of newsstands that carry *Playboy*?"

He smiled and confessed, and I saw that the topic was not going to die easy. Or, come to think of it, why should it? Wasn't the beautiful woman and her undraped body one of life's sweetest and most perplexing temptations?

"Edward, I understand," I told him. "I share your interest. We're lucky there are so many pretty women, and it's natural to wonder what they look like without clothes. But my answer has to be, you're much too young." Other reservations I held against "girlie" magazines I kept to myself.

"Dad," he pleaded, "my birthday's coming up. Could I please get a subscription to *Playboy* as my best gift?"

I thought back to when Edward was four and how he loved to pore over the nudes in *The Family of Man* collection and how we'd pause in front of pharmacies to study the photographs of the nearly naked French women advertising suntan lotion. I remembered when I was a youngster and *Life* published a picture of a woman standing by a swimming pool wearing what the magazine predicted would cause a revolution in swim wear, a new style called the bikini. By today's standards, the costume was modest. The bottom even had a little skirt. But you could see the woman's midriff and even her navel. I became infatuated with that tiny, shadowy circle. I found tracing paper and made endless outlines of the woman, and when I got to the belly button I tickled her with my pencil. For a long time I kept the original photograph tucked away in my underwear drawer. The only other exciting pictures available to me were on the covers of detective magazines—women in their bras and panties about to be slaughtered by fiends. What's the sense of getting interested, I figured, when they're going to be a dead bloody mess in a few minutes.

So, because it also was my feeling, I felt my son's excitement and pleasure and anxiety. But I told him no again on the magazine as kindly as I knew how, and after a few more nights of asking he let the subject drop.

A short time later our house was opened to an overnight stay by a half-dozen Cub Scouts. It was chaos, as I had expected, with the sounds of thundering feet up and down the staircase half the night, and voices coming from the television set at 4:00 AM, and my sleepwalking to the door and barking, "Shut off that dirty show and get some rest!"

In the morning I found the stalwart Scouts strewn about the living room, all of them in deep and exhausted slumber. But what caught my eye was a small collection of postcards that evidentially had been passed around during the night. They belonged to Edward but had come from me. I hadn't realized until that moment how important they were to him. They included photographs of nude statues from the Museum of Modern Art, one of a woman who might have been naked about to enter the surf, with the message, "Greetings from Cape Cod," and, the only lascivious one, an illustration of a voluptuous, sloe-eyed woman, looking back at the viewer, her thumbs hooked around the last scrap of her clothing and about to be peeled off. This postcard was at the top of the bunch and obviously had been the Scouts' favorite.

I once played a prank with a copy of the same card. A man in an office where I worked at the time often intimated that he led an untamed sex life away from home and conducted many of his conquests at a mysterious site only a few blocks away. Soon afterward, on a lunchtime walk, I was approached by a man giving out postcards, which he slapped against his free hand for emphasis. It was the lascivious woman with an invitation to meet her at a topless club called something like Adam Meets Eve. I wrote on the cards, "Dear Ralph, Missed you yesterday, XXX Tina" and put it in the mail. A few days later Ralph, suspecting me, blurted out, "My secretary saw that card and that message, and the whole mailroom saw it, too, for God's sakes!" I felt bad that my attempt to moralize had backfired but never confessed that I'd been the culprit.

Viewing the card again and the tender faces of the Scouts made me pause and wonder just how far I'd come since I traced the woman in the bikini. It also forced me to realize I'd yet to come to grips with the Albany motel room.

Our whole family had gone to Albany for an overnight visit, and while my wife attended a school board conference, the three children and I explored a new city. As we were packing the next morning, I compulsively opened every drawer in our room and found, instead of the perennial Gideon Bible, a magazine left by some lonesome Samaritan. I thumbed through it quickly and hid it in my duffle bag.

Back at home, I was the boy again with the forbidden magazine. Now the drawer contained my binoculars and seldom-used assortment of pocket handkerchiefs, a lint brush, several belts and pairs of suspenders—and the motel room surprise. I began on occasion flipping through the pages, not without excitement.

But wait a minute. If I were going to be honest with Edward, I had to be honest with myself. Did I have the right to keep that magazine? And, on a less lofty plane, what if my son caught me with it? When the Scouts had departed and the house was quiet, I rolled it up, slipped an elastic band around it and buried it deep in the kitchen garbage pail.

But just before I did, I opened the magazine one last time, to this glorious brunette. She's in the jungle, see, and it has become excruciatingly hot, so she doffs her pith helmet and unbuttons her safari jacket. And then those heavy chino knickers have to go and, sure enough, one thing leads to another.

Language

A crude intruder one day invaded the tranquil airwaves of our blissful domicile. It went: "Aw, shut up … I hate you … you stupid … jerk!"

The sound became so patently unpleasant that I decided economic sanctions against bad language had to be imposed. The unanimous vote was taken by both parents, who comprise the family board, over the loud and virtually anarchistic protests of the family members—boys, ages nine and ten, and a girl, age seven. My wife never did reveal the name of the chairperson of our board, but she did appoint me chief of the language police.

The banned expressions were not selected lightly but only following an exasperating sampling of all the questionable language slung at and around each other. I felt we'd hit etymological pay dirt the day I announced the ban. "That's stupid, Dad," said one of the boys, serving as negotiator for his entire generation.

"Twenty-five cents, please," I replied calmly, palm extended. The others laughed and one of them said, "He caught you easy enough, Edward."

Edward glared and said, "Aw, shut up, Charles."

"That'll be twenty-five cents, Edward," said Sara, gleefully.

Stunned by dissension in his own ranks, Edward sputtered at his sister, "I hate you, you jerk."

"A double! Fifty cents!" bubbled Charles, happy not to be the offender.

At this pace, I thought, I could take early retirement.

It was never so easy again, however. The children quickly learned to check themselves when one of the Big Four began to roll itself across their little tongues, at least in my earshot. They even developed refinements, insisting on what they labeled an "exception"—a time-out when one of the offending words was permissible because no other word fit the moment as well.

Upon reflection I agreed with them. When a man in a jammed elevator crowed to a companion about his brilliant business scheme, was he not a jerk, conceivably a stupid jerk? And when a child set out to rig the game of hide-and-seek so that there was a victim, a little kid who was always "it," was not this manipulator also a jerk?

What I did not allow to develop was a snitcher–snitchee relationship. "Dad, Sara said three shut-ups today" might earn the snitcher a one-time penalty for uttering the word "shut-ups," but usually I let both get away with a warning. The jackpot—a whole buck for all of the words in the same intemperate sentence—became a pipedream, for the plan worked well. After a while, earnings of the Big Four Fund dropped off to a trickle—fifty or seventy-five cents for the entire week.

Knowing the incredible cleverness of children, I took the eldest aside one day and asked if bad language was way down in the house or way down only when I was home. He reflected on the question and replied, almost to his own surprise, that language habits had indeed improved.

Wouldn't you know it, just as I was contemplating a lifting of the sanctions, a three-headed conspiracy bearded me one evening. "We've decided," said the spokeschild, "that the twenty-five-cent penalty should work both ways or not at all. It isn't fair for us to pay you if you don't pay us."

"Very good, children," I said, mildly amused, "but there are things you don't understand. For one thing, I'm the parent. A lot happens that would upset me, oblige me to use on occasion one or more of the Big Four." Examples, please, said three sets of litigious eyes.

"The Ku Klux Klan. They dress up in sheets and hoods and talk about how they hate certain kinds of people."

"Okay. But after you hung up the phone the other night, you said the man was—Dad, exception—you said he was a stupid jerk."

"Yes, yes, that's because he couldn't get it through his thick skull that I had no interest in winning a week at his Caribbean nudist camp or whatever it was."

"We don't see the difference. When you get upset, you're allowed to say the bad words. When we get upset, it costs us money."

I pondered their point for a long silent time while staring at a patch of discolored paint on the ceiling. After that I rubbed my eyes, carefully placed the bookmark in my book and set it down. Then I looked into each face and knew I finally had to say something. "Aw, shut up," I explained. Three smiling faces watched as I fished in my pocket for the money.

Clowns

My three children have been in school now for a total of more than fifteen years. I knew it was only a matter of time before the reappearance of the family affliction. It is not sinister. Of all the burdens, doubts and peculiarities that I lugged through childhood and into my adult years, it was the only one I didn't want to give up.

Most children have a favorite blanket or stuffed toy, the so-called security blanket. I had one. I toddled around with mine, a blue-and-red wool plaid, until it was reduced to a tattered scrap of two square inches. But one day I misplaced it and never needed it again.

Not true of the family condition. Since families are supposed to be forgiving and friends tolerant, the habit surfaces where spontaneity is not always at a premium—in the classroom. That is what happened to me, and that, I felt, would happen sooner or later to one or more of my children.

I arrived home one recent day to find my wife, who has gained local fame for her cheerfulness, in a fretful mood. "The report cards came today," she said, in tones so measured by control that I suspected our children had been assessed as incorrigible nitwits and reformatory candidates. Reaching for the reports, I read up and down the columns. Some had done better than others, but all had achieved respectable grades. It was the comment penned by the teacher of our oldest child, who is eleven, that had disturbed my wife. It read:

"Edward has been taking it too easy this quarter. He is often silly and distracts others."

That was it. I was disappointed to hear that he might be coasting through school. But the important thing was that he had finally begun to clown.

"The family curse!" I said. "It's finally surfaced in the current generation. I was beginning to think we'd never see it again!"

My wife looked puzzled. I could have sworn she was about to say that I act silly enough for the entire family, but when she saw my pride she relaxed and began to smile.

"What other honorable choice does a little boy or girl have in the regimentation of school," I asked her, "but to challenge the seriousness, the pomposity, the tyranny of the adults with a little well-aimed clowning? It's what got me through school."

"What you may see as ideal emotional health," said my beautiful alter ego, "the teacher may see as the calculated mischief of a wise guy."

"No, the family affliction does not involve cruel pranks or hurting someone's feelings," I responded. "It only allows you to let off steam—lighten up, as people say these days—when a situation is too much to bear."

Lest my wife think I was fabricating family history on the spot, I reminded her: "You know my mother loves a daily dose of fun. Growing up in Toronto, she had to carry the burden for her whole family—nine kids, plus the two parents. That's a lot of clowning, especially in Canada, where until very recently there were ordinances against it."

The school bus arrived, and three professional noisemakers entered by the kitchen door and decorated the living room with knapsacks, important educational advisories crushed into aeronautic experiments, and uneaten lunches undergoing gruesome metamorphoses under waxed paper. I congratulated all on their academic prowess, noticing that Edward hung back. He excused himself as quickly as possible and went upstairs to his room. He knew the teacher's remark was coming. It had circled him like a furious insect and finally stung.

I left him to shift about his room, check out his baseball-card collection, and maybe peer out the window with his binoculars to the treetops and the hills in the distance, and then I headed up.

When I knocked and entered he looked a little scared. I asked if anything dramatic had transpired in class. "No, Dad," he said, and went on to describe the mood of the classroom.

"Edward, I may be a grumpy old adult sometimes, but you have to admit I like a laugh. Even your friends, and they are one tough audience, say I'm funny. The fact is, when I was in school, I was the class clown. I'm talking about the first grade and the fifth [which is his grade] and the twelfth grade and even college. Being silly was the family trademark. I was the only one in my family to inherit it. You may be the lucky one in your generation."

His eyes widened. "You want an example? Some kids were sneaking cigarettes. They smoked in the schoolyard. They challenged me to smoke, and called me 'chicken' when I refused to take a 'drag.' I rarely backed off from a challenge but I didn't want to smoke, I was training to become a U.S. Olympic sprinter some day. So I whipped out a snack. I took a bite of my graham cracker and then tapped it with my finger and the crumbs fell off, like ashes dropping. That's the way I started to eat them. After a while, everyone was smoking cookies, flicking crumbs at each other and laughing. Some teachers enjoyed it; some made speeches on attracting vermin. They may still be doing it. That's the legacy I left the school."

Edward tapped his thumb with his forefinger, recognizing the habit I maintain to this day. I was touched by the apprentice imitating the master.

"I don't know if you can get this one. This is the curse at work at the mental level. In college, a professor tried to embarrass me by asking a certain question. I don't know why, but he had it in for me. He had been talking about 'truisms' and suddenly he said, 'Mr. Hadad, can you tell the class what a truism is?'

"I stood up, thought for a moment, and said, 'Yes.' He nodded for me to continue. 'A truism is a remark attributed to Harry S Truman.'

"That wasn't the right answer. A truism is simply a very well-known statement, which may or may not be actually true. Harry S Truman was a president before you were born. But the question called for a silly answer, and I gave it to him. The class, of course, found it hilarious."

Edward looked a little puzzled. "Maybe you had to be there. But the point is the same. You have the right to have fun. It's guaranteed in the Constitution of the United States."

"Daaaad ..."

"Let me tell you this and believe every word of it. I am proud of you. I am proud that you sometimes clown around. It is healthy. It is a family tradition. And never let anyone talk you out of it." I hugged him then and, as he was getting to be a big boy, he got his arms around me and hugged me back.

"What are you men talking about up there?" my wife asked, when she saw us together. "I hope you got something straightened out."

Edward shot me a grin. "Don't be silly, Mom," he said. My boy, he had arrived.

Carnival

The woman leaned out of her second-story window. "Why don't you take them to the carnival? All kids love a carnival." She was mourning her husband of thirty years, the end of a union that had produced no children, though in her sadness and kindness and simplicity, she was childlike herself. A few months earlier she had intercepted my wife and me and our three youngsters as we approached my parents' door for a visit, introduced herself by her first name, and poured out her story. This time she had new sad tidings. She had fallen and broken a leg. When she described the accident, she smiled so broadly I thought she would burst into laughter. Then she mentioned the carnival and her own inability to attend. I expressed my sympathy and thanked her for her advice.

As it turned out we were at loose ends the very next evening. My wife wanted to stay home and visit with my parents. The children, after a formal restaurant dinner, were fidgety and ripe for adventure. Lightly I ordered them to the car, and we set out on the streets I used to know well in my old hometown. "Where to, Dad?" They wanted to know. I remained mysterious, just in case I couldn't locate the fair and told them only to keep watching the skyline. We chatted back seat to front, and I took great pleasure in the completeness of their companionship. Edward Salim, at age ten provided many observations and insights that had eluded me. It was he, for instance, who insisted I dismiss a hurt caused by an old friend and give him another chance. Edward's brother and sister, age nine and six, have wisdom of their own.

I swung across the streets and up roads almost on instinct, but once we reached Centre Street I could almost sense the carnival. And, sure enough, there in the distant lavender sky at dusk, like a saucerful of stars, were the lights of the Ferris wheel. "As your beloved old man is fond of saying," I announced triumphantly, "Look up, my children, always look up."

They chirped with anticipation and a few minutes later, after I delivered severe warnings on the importance of staying together, we entered upon the magical grounds of a neighborhood carnival. Compressed onto a vacant lot, down the street from the public library and across from the firehouse, the carnival was bright and noisy, the air filled with the smells of frying dough and sausage and sizzling onions, a place to dare and dream and die a little of fright before heading home and wondering why every day could not be as thrilling.

The children were allowed to spend several dollars at games that remained remarkably unchanged since I was a boy: squirting water into the mouth of a plaster clown until a balloon burst over his head or knocking three lead milk bottles off a platform with a baseball. The only difference was, when I was young, the men operating the games seemed adventurous and the women glamorous. Now they merely looked bored and tough.

We purchased tickets for the rides, and I watched with both amusement and awe as my three gems rose into the sky in the swaying compartment of the Ferris wheel. Edward looked tense. His brother Charles Aram shut his eyes. Sara Jameela, the baby of the three, alone peered around with glee on her face and waved down at me. When they returned, I asked how it had gone, and no one would admit to anything beyond pure pleasure.

They tried other rides. We paused for cotton candy. I didn't know it could be blue as well as pink. And then they found the ride that would transport them with excitement. It was called The Scrambler and resembled a mechanical octopus with small gondolas attached to the end of each tentacle. When the man in the old-fashioned rimless glasses and coveralls squeezed the grips of the controls and set the ride in motion, the cars began to move slowly around, slightly undulating, but then picking up speed, whiplashing and tossing the revolving cars in the most unexpected directions. Riders screamed with fear and surprise. The very thought of going on almost made me sick, but the children were eager.

They waited in line and were soon aboard, each, in an independence that grows daily, taking a separate car. The ride started up, and I watched and waved and spun my head in every which way trying to follow them. It was clear they were crazy about the ride. My eye caught another rider, a good-looking young man with red hair wearing a violet shirt and grey trousers. His arms, which were curiously underdeveloped, were pulled against his chest as he buried his face in his hands. He'll be glad when this is over, but what a rough way to learn a lesson, I thought.

The octopus became weary when the man in the glasses squeezed the switch again, and my children came racing back to me, insisting they must go on again. I agreed they could. The ride came alive and to my amazement, there was the man with the red hair and the violet shirt. Only this time his thin arms were raised outward, in celebration, and he waved them in unison, fists closed, to express his joy. When the ride came to a stop this time, he alighted quickly and was gone from sight. I imagined he was lining up to buy still more tickets. I realized then he was mentally retarded. I shed a tear, comparing his lot with that of my three God-given treasures.

It was long after nightfall and, despite their touching protests, I told the children it was time to return home to see Mom and the grandparents. On the way they began the inevitable game of comparing what they had liked most about the carnival. Edward's choice filled me with wonderment. "Did you see the man on The Scrambler in a purple shirt?" he asked.

"Yes," I answered tentatively, "what about him?"

"I felt happy for that man," Edward said.

Making Room on the Pedestal

We are out for a drive, the three children and I. It is one of my favorite times. It renders me noble in the eyes of their mother, who gets a dearly earned breather. The motion of the car, the passing landscape, the chatter that ping-pongs back seat to front, the trumped-up importance of our errand—all bring excitement to the ride. It also makes my two young sons and daughter spontaneous, outspoken.

"Dad knows everything in the whole world, don't you, Dad?" ventures eight-year-old Edward. The temptation to agree is tremendous. I find myself making compromises with the truth that would not serve me well in the adult world: "Well, children, I do know a lot of things, but it isn't quite right to say I know everything."

Charles, age seven, wields a crayon over a pad, and I observe through the rear-view mirror that he is jotting something down. "Dad, what did I just write?" he asks.

"Lincoln's Gettysburg Address or the Emancipation Proclamation."

"Wrong. I did a 'D.'"

"That only shows," interjects Edward, "that Dad doesn't know everything but he still knows almost everything."

Sara, five, seems content to play with a gaudily dressed doll, all pink yarn and yellow curls, that we found at a garage sale.

"How is Sally Sweet feeling today?" I ask her.

"This isn't Sally Sweet," she replies with good-natured impatience, "this is Suzy Sunshine."

I forget that things can change, that Sally Sweet was yesterday, and I apologize to Sara and to Suzy, and all is well.

Sara believes that I am the toughest, bravest, most loving dad in the history of dadhood. That is because I've worked so hard to convince her of it. When she came home from nursery school one time complaining that a boy had poked her in one of her glorious brown eyes, I was ripping to call the parents, give the boy's old man a good pop in his eye, challenge the competency of the school, clear the whole place out, get its license yanked. "You're the best daddy in the whole wide world" was Sara's response to my diatribe.

Yet I feel intimations of my limits and start to wonder if the children are catching on. They like to climb aboard my shoulders and, clutching me in a virtual stranglehold, be taken on rides from room to room. The outlook from my shoulders—even taller than their dad—fills them with giddy joy. But recently I stopped lifting the boys. They know they're growing, are proud of their bodies, but don't quite understand why their powerful and brilliant dad won't play Horsey or Camel anymore.

A few months earlier my right elbow began to hurt severely. Tendonitis, said the doctor, like tennis elbow. I couldn't even strut that I'd been hurt in a heroic singles match. I'd got the problem from over-enthusiasm in pulling weeds.

I thought back to my college years and my brief, picaresque career as a prizefighter. My hands were so fast I was asked to spar with the welterweight champion. After obtaining somewhat humiliating assurances that the champ would not hit back but only try to deflect my punches, I entered the ring with him. We went three rounds, and I pasted him good a couple of times.

Last summer, in the middle of an attempt to resume jogging, something snapped as I ran up the stairs from the Lexington Avenue subway to Forty-Second Street. I'd only been running ten-minute workouts; a few years before I'd finished twenty-six-mile marathons in New York and on Long Island. My left knee swelled up angrily; the running comeback—although there would be others—was over.

I arrive at the decision that I must give the children other heroes. On holidays I begin telling them about the American soldiers and sailors, thousands and thousands of them, brave and decent men and women, who had to go far away to fight wars so that we could live free, without bad people and wise guys pushing us around and telling us what to do. I tell them that many of those Americans had to die to get the job done. I tell them how important their teachers are, how much they can learn if they pay attention, if they show respect by not wearing jeans to school.

"But teachers aren't always right, are they, Dad?" Charles asks.

"You are right," I tell him, "you couldn't be more right. Teachers don't have all the answers, and no one else does, either. This may come as a shocker, children, but not even your amazing dad is right all the time."

I wait for them to protest, and no one does.

Edward one evening picks up a heavy book I'd been going through, a collection of stories. He reads well enough to ask, "Who's John Cheever?"

"A terrific writer, a wonderful writer who happened to die a few years ago. If I were as good as he I could go upstairs for a while every day and write and support our whole family very nicely."

"Saturdays, too?" he wants to know.

"Absolutely not. That would still belong to us and our rides."

I announce one day to the children that if they are incredibly good, Mom and I will take them to the big circus in the Nassau Coliseum. Sara and Charles cheer wildly, but Edward only smiles. He has seen the word "circus" written on the calendar by my wife Evelyn so he even knows what day we'll attend.

The circus, just as it's supposed to be, is frantic and bewildering with activity. I marvel at it through their eyes. They eat and drink and ruminate and gape and absorb with such endearing fullness that I begin to feel I'm sharing the children with the performers. In a lull, I head up the concrete steps, and when I return everyone is grateful for the popcorn, and my knee is throbbing.

We witness a man named Miguel Vasquez complete four somersaults off a flying trapeze and be caught by his partner hanging upside down. It is breathtaking. When Vasquez first did the stunt in public it was page-one news.

Another man, Wade Burck, enters a cage containing fifteen tigers. Before he is done, he is riding one tiger while another leaps through a hoop of flame held over his head.

A man in a jumpsuit and white helmet waves to the crowd, then removes his helmet and enters the cannon barrel, to be shot across three rings and land in a net. "Captain Christopher!" cheers the ringmaster.

Charles asks afterward: "Why did he take his helmet off when he went into the cannon?" Nobody can guess.

As we shuffle out with the rest of the audience, the children, now exhausted, use their last gasp of energy to deliver agitated judgments on their favorite performance. Evelyn leans into them and whispers something. A moment later there's a monotone chorus: "Thank you, Dad."

We are driving home, my wife at the wheel, the children asleep. An hour later we are in our driveway. It is late and dark and cold, and we hustle to open the house, turn up the heat, turn down the beds, and get the children in. Evelyn has Sara out of the car and into her bed while I ready the boys' bunks. They're stretched out dreamily in the back of the station wagon, under covers. I tug at them, coax them. "Let's go, my big boys; let's get inside and into bed. You're much too big for Dad to carry. I know it's not easy, you're as tired as can be, try and do it for Daddio."

For the first time I can remember, each dutifully opens his eyes and slides from the wagon and starts walking, first tentatively, then determinedly, to the house. I hold their hands and guide them on the steps to the second floor, fearing they may fall. They sense my help but make it to bed under their own steam.

A new kind of feeling settles over me as Evelyn and I take a sip of late-night wine, and I describe it to her. It is a feeling of a burden lifted, bittersweet but satisfying. It is a feeling that I'm still the children's hero, but from now on I'll be sharing the honor with Miguel Vasquez and John Cheever and teachers and soldiers and others who will come along.

Evelyn says nothing but smiles warmly and raises her glass in preparation for a toast. I raise mine and say: "To the new guys on the pedestal."

Freedom Ride

Fiery steeds, nostrils flaring, speed away, carrying my children with them. The children shout and fling their fists in the air, but I have no fear for their safety. I know I will see them again in less than a minute. Still, no amount of coaxing can get me to join them on the merry-go-round.

The eldest of the three children is ten. When I was ten, I loved the merry-go-round. Even at five, I remembered my father, in his brown suit and broad tie and felt hat with the tiny gray feather, poised by the side of my dipping and rearing horse, prepared to catch me if I toppled from the saddle (which I never did). My mother stood behind the safety line, her hand raised in a dainty wave and her anxious smile concealing a prayer.

The fancier the merry-go-round, the greater the excitement. The ones with arrangements of mirrors and light bulbs and painted scenes of gypsy camps above wildly colored horses and carriages were the best. From the center of it all, from an exotic cluster of gold-painted pipes and whistles, rose the melodic din of the calliope. Like most children, I bolted from the safety of the fairy-tale carriages almost as soon as I was able to run. They were for infants and grandparents. Some of my friends at the beach—for that was where the great amusement park was located, at the edge of the ocean—chose favorite horses and even gave them names. I had a favorite too, cream-colored, with a flying mane of red and blue and a saddle of shiny black, but I didn't name him. Why bother, I thought solemnly, when the park will soon be deserted and boarded up for winter, and all of us children will be far away, fidgeting in overheated classrooms?

My children are different. Every cat or dog or polliwog or stuffed animal that comes their way is honored with a name. Sara, who is seven, persuaded her grandmother to purchase a stuffed blue bear, so large it fills a corner of her room. I took an immediate dislike to the enormity of it, until she came to me at bedtime, hefting the bear, and said, "Night, Daddy. Blueberry and I are tired."

My long aversion to merry-go-rounds, I kept secret from my wife and children, and I never evaded taking them to carnivals and fairs and amusement parks. One park, like the one of my boyhood, was by the sea. I bought them tickets and watched them scramble for horses, but when the merry-go-round began to move and the calliope to pipe its song, my pleasure was over. The music, intended to be simple and cheerful, was haunting instead.

Merry-go-rounds suggested lost youth—whether squandered, forfeited or abandoned, or all or none of those—irretrievably lost. I wondered was the merry-go-round, like life itself, a ride from which the fortunate grab handfuls of brass rings while the rest continue on around and around? That thought made my melancholy all the more mysterious, for I have caught more than my share of brass rings, not the least of which is my family.

A chilly autumn Sunday afternoon found all of us spent and listless. To avoid yet another round of cooking, my wife called a pizzeria three miles away and asked me to fetch the food. Sara agreed to come along. When we arrived, the pizzas were not yet ready, and we wandered over to a school playground. It contained a few swings and beams for climbing and, most intriguing, a simple merry-go-round, a scarred and battered wooden base balanced on an unseen mechanism and, in place of horses and carriages, a circle of iron pipes to hold on to.

Sara seized a pipe and raced around until it seemed the merry-go-round would lift her off the ground. Only then did she leap aboard and begin her ride. When the merry-go-round slowed, she called for me to rebuild its speed. After a while it slowed again, and she jumped off. "Daddy, now it's your turn. You get on and I'll give you a ride," she said.

"No," I replied, "the merry-go-round's for children. You take one more ride and we'll get the food and head home."

She jumped on again and I began to run with the lumbering contraption. When it reached a high speed, I stood back and watched Sara, her head tossed back, eyes aflame with pleasure. Then something strange happened. I leaped aboard and looked up at the swirling sycamore branches and the schoolhouse windows and the rooftops and the sky behind them and felt queasy and giddy.

"Sara!" I shouted. "What's the name of your horse?"

She looked puzzled for a moment, then patted the pipe she was grasping and said, "Pepperoni! What's yours?"

"Anchovy!" I told her. I could hardly wait for summer to come.

Choosing

It is bedtime, and Edward, who is eleven, approaches. "G'night, Dad," he says and offers a kiss on the lips. Charles, a year younger and discreet since babyhood, is next and allows me to peck his cheek. Then the last, Sara, who is eight and has confided to my wife that Dad doesn't always smell that great, especially after taking a drink. I get to kiss her somewhere between the crown of her head and the nape of her neck. My wife Evelyn, who is very smart and very sentimental, watches, and there is in her smile something resembling adoration. A moment later she is accorded the same tokens of affection, and the children are gone.

"Is it just me or do you find yourself sometimes wondering which one you love the most?" I ask her lazily. It is a late-night kind of thought, silly and serious in the same breath.

Evelyn hesitates, confused by the question. "I find it crazy, impossible to answer," she says. "It's a dreadful question in a way, like the German officer in *Sophie's Choice* insisting she decide which of her two children she will send to the concentration camp in order to save the other."

"I'm not condemning any of my children," I protest, suddenly aware of the intensity of the subject.

The fact is, the question does return, and I find myself searching my brain or my heart for an answer. I pause and say hesitantly, "I happen to have a favorite."

"Who?" she demands to know.

"It's Charles. I love them all, of course, but I've found myself loving him so much recently. Maybe it's because he's the middle child, as I was, and I am seeing resemblances, seeing myself in my boy. Or maybe it's his sweet, helpful manner. You know how the others bicker over who spilled the juice or who left the bikes out in the rain. He's the one who shows up at my worktable with a sliced peach and a bowl of popcorn and that glorious smile and says, 'Have a snack, Dad.'

"I'll tell you another thing," I continue. "A few nights ago when I was up at three in the morning, an irrational thought came over me. What if we lost Charles? And I wondered if I would want to live without him."

The memory stuns me and alarms Evelyn, and I quickly add, "I know it's nonsense, darling. But that didn't stop the thought from popping into my head."

"So Charles is your favorite?" she asks. There is in her question an accusation, a suggestion that I have wronged two children by preferring a third.

"Yes and no. I keep switching." I laugh because her motherly anger has chased away the momentary gloom. "I'm crazy about Edward. Some days he's my favorite. You know how the older kids on the school bus can't wait to razz the younger ones. That doesn't stop Edward the Kisser. He knows they're all watching out the bus windows, and he kisses me, almost brazenly, as if to say, nothing comes between my dad and me, not even you bozos.

"As for Sara, she has been a joy since the second she appeared and the delivery-room nurses cooed, 'It's a girl, it's a girl.' We've been taking our walks in the woods and having our talks since she was two. I cherish every moment with her. And you know I hold her in special affection for another reason: you produced three wonderful children, but two of them are fair, like you. Sara is my dark beauty, dark-haired like me. Yes, she is my favorite too."

My wife then admits that the same question that ambushes me has passed through her head. "But I dismissed it as unanswerable," she tells me, smugly.

Still, I intuitively know I am not alone in my folly. Everyone you meet has an opinion on whether he or she was the most loved child in the household.

"Were you the favorite in your family?" I ask Evelyn, who has two sisters and a brother.

"No," she says comfortably and remembers how she was brought up to believe there was only one royal child, her brother, the prince. She asks about me.

"I don't really know. I'm not troubled by it. My sister claims I was the favorite. I suspect she was. And our younger brother, he probably got more special attention than either of us."

In the bright clarity of a morning soon afterward, at breakfast, Edward suddenly asks me with a smile, "Who do you love the most?"

Had he heard our conversation? I wonder. Does he feel that as the eldest he is the choice? At any rate, he has confidence to ask the question.

"Let's see. That's a tough one," I reply. "You, I guess. No, wait. I think it must be Charles. No, upon reflection, it's got to be Sara. Oh, now you've got me confused."

I turn to my wife, who looks wary. I turn back to the children and began to tell them I love them all equally. But something stops me. "It is a very interesting question, and I'm prepared to give you an honest answer," I say.

"C'mon, Dad, quit stalling," says Edward.

"Your mother," I tell them. "I love you all, but I love her the most. That's the way it's supposed to be."

Evelyn is both tense and pleased. A few moments pass. I kiss and nuzzle the children, and they become relaxed and reassured. They have done me an enormous favor. They have forced me to answer my own perplexing question. I grew up a lot that morning. So did we all.

Jenkins the Cat

I spotted the cat at the other side of the road, poised to bolt. I slammed on the brakes but my front wheel caught it, and a pleasant day in the suburbs was plunged into confusion and gloom. Pulling onto a shoulder, I walked back to the spot. The cat, which had a luxurious white coat and blue eyes, had hobbled from the road to a driveway and lay on its side, seemingly crying beyond sound. I knelt and felt it and was afraid to move it. Its collar read "Jenkins."

A car pulled up containing two women, and one got out and peered at the cat. "Broken leg, nothing too serious. Get it to the animal hospital," she said.

I looked up at her. "Where? Where?" She tossed a hand over her shoulder toward the nearby village of Briarcliff Manor, got back in the car and was driven away.

I left the cat and went to a house and knocked and rang. A boy's face appeared at pulled-back curtains. "Where do the Jenkinses live?" I shouted through the glass. "I hit their cat. I need to find them!"

He came outside, saying the name was unfamiliar, and walked me back to the cat. "He's dying," said the boy, who was about twelve years old. "They shouldn't let him out like that. I recognize him now. Jenkins is *his* name." The boy told me where his owners lived.

The boy's sister alighted from a school bus and joined us. She was fascinated and appalled by the cat. It suddenly twitched severely, and as it became still its lips peeled back to reveal pointy teeth. "Don't feel bad, Mister," said the girl. "It wasn't your fault." The two of them left.

A police car cruised by but I didn't flag it down. I didn't know what to say to them.

I reached under the cat and cradled it in both arms and walked toward the house where I was told it had lived. I felt as though I was leading a procession.

At the front door the mat read, "Go Away." I wished I could. I placed the cat down at the front of the steps leading to the house and knocked front and back. The house was empty. I returned to my car for paper and pencil and found none and drove the two miles to my house.

My three young children were just home from school and playing outdoors. "A terrible thing happened," I told them. "I killed a cat."

Charles's face darkened. He is seven. "I'm getting ready to cry; I love Megan," he said. When he said "love" his pronunciation carried traces of his infancy and it came out "wuv."

I said it was a different cat. They seemed relieved but pressed for details and then went in search of Megan. I went inside and looked up the number and dialed Jenkins's house.

"Hello?" said a boy's voice. It was deeper than a child's but not yet a man's and it was brimming with sobs. I could not bring myself to say I'd killed his cat so I said instead, "It was my car that ran over your cat. I'm very sorry."

"Thank you for calling. It was kind of you," the boy said.

"I only live up the road, I want to leave my name and number in case you or your family want to reach me. I can't tell you how bad I feel."

"There's no need for that information. Really," he said, but he listened as I told him who I was and where to find me. We hung up.

The children found me in the cellar puttering. "Are you crying, Dad?" one asked. "Because you killed the cat?"

"Yes. The boy who owned it loved it and was very sad. And he was so polite and decent on the phone."

I asked my wife if I could be excused from the afternoon's activities and get away by myself, a request more imposing than it might sound because she had been depending on me to give her a little relief from the children. She agreed. I knew exactly what I wanted to do and put the tackle in the car and headed for the nearby Tarrytown Lakes.

For several hours I cast and retrieved, comforted by the familiar action and setting. I watched the changes in the patterns of the water and the sky and thought of Jenkins and did not want to get any strikes.

I stayed until the sun began to set behind the sand-colored building of Marymount College in the distance, conjuring Jerusalem at dusk, and returned home.

The solace of the lakes departed, however, as I became convinced I'd be receiving a bitter telephone call. I paced most of the evening, rejecting my nightly cocktail, wanting to be fully alert, getting the jitters whenever the phone rang, experiencing dread.

The phone call did not come that night. It never came. Ultimately, I could not help but feel the boy and his family expressed their love for Jenkins by forgiving me.

New Car

There are certain dreads that must be universal among men: the dread of turning and running on a battlefield; the dread that a desirable woman will look you straight in the eye and whisper, "Not so long as you shall live"; and the dread of the first scratch on your brand-new automobile.

Who is to say which is the most painful? I refrain from tales of personal valor on the ground that I have heard a hundred and not believed a single one. Any discussion of desirable women I have or have not known or hope to know could provoke yet another dread— that of destroying my domestic tranquility and with it the gossamer illusion that I came to our union a spiritual virgin. But having owned a good half-dozen brand-new cars, I consider myself fully qualified to discourse on the topic of scratch dread.

Earlier models I've owned I will mention only in passing. I once had a brand-new Opel. In those days lots of people still harbored strong feelings about World War II and the Axis powers. Bringing home my German sedan from the dealer, I—for the first and, I hope, last time in my life—was booed for driving down my own block. The first scratch was perpetrated several days later. We suspected a Veteran of Foreign Wars member, out on night patrol, but no one confessed or was apprehended.

Another car I didn't own long enough to scratch because it was forced off the road by Ralph Nader. It was beautiful and sleek, a black Corvair with red imitation-leather bucket seats and a jaunty floor shift. But Ralph said to leap from the Corvair before it fishtailed you into the graveyard.

The pert Peugeot 304, which I loved with the abandon of an American in Paris, got scratched in the cosmic sense; it was broken in half in a long-ago divorce settlement. The redwood Chevy wagon, a.k.a. Malibu Classic, took its first scratch in the flank from a runaway supermarket cart.

But the dread became personal, intimate, with my latest brand-new car because this car was meant for me, and I meant to keep it perfect. She was a cute little Nissan. The dealer called her "silver" but between us, the color was gray. She had some flash—a blue racing stripe, black matte bumpers and door guards. But inside she was pure and good and simple, with a no-nonsense, five-speed manual transmission. Her only optional frill was an AM-FM radio, which the dealer called "digital" because you had to poke buttons with a digit (your finger) to bring in a station.

I put our three children in the back seat and my wife Evelyn up front with me, and we sat there on the gravel-covered lot and never bothered to take a test ride. The dealer saw the "I'll take it" look in my eyes and said we could pick her up in three days. Easing onto the highway for the premiere ride—across the county and into our driveway—I began to feel a kind of gnawing sensation that spread from heart to stomach, wondering from where that first scratch would come.

We arrived home unscathed, and I spent that first day studying her body and its perfection. Even nature's dust from a nearby dogwood I brushed away moments after it landed on her roof or hood.

I began leaving my Nissan at a suburban train station most mornings. Returning in the evenings, I'd dash to her and inspect every surface. The children, under the threat of spending the summer in bed, were ordered to avoid the car at all times.

"How can we avoid it if you ask us to sit in the back?" asked one wise guy. "I'll put you in blindfolded," I told him. Megan the cat, a part of the family for the last two years, picked up the habit of gently negotiating the roof, where she would sit serenely, like the sculptured cats of ancient Egypt. I enjoyed the pose, partly because it turned my plain but beautiful new car into a kind of regal tableau.

All went well and the initial gnawing dread-of-scratch dissipated. That is, until one otherwise glorious summer evening after I'd come outdoors, martini in hand, to enjoy the dusk. One of the children came running, anguish pinching his perfect little features. "Megan scratched the trunk of your brand-new car!" he blurted out and then raced back to the scene of the infamy. Incredulous at first, I painstakingly lowered my martini, another sacred object after all, and ran after him.

There were, alas, two distinct sets of long, thin scratches as the herald/child had claimed. I gasped and began to rub my fingers over the desecration, pitifully hoping the marks were a grease smudge or even a trick of the late day's light and shadow. They were not. And peering down from the roof, calm and aloof, sat Megan.

"Regal, my foot!" I shouted, and I reached up and swung a roundhouse punch. It packed lethal power and was intended to. But the cat leaped out of range, in the act striking and snapping off the Nissan's radio antenna, and fled into the woods.

"One minute I had a brand-new car; now all I've got is a pile of junk!" I wailed. Evelyn came running from the house, quickly assessed the damage to the car and my mental health and began to say soothing words. Our relationship, the bond between my Nissan and me, was never the same after that evening. Was it worse than turning tail in battle or being told by a beautiful woman to shove off? I don't know for sure, but once an animal has scratched your brand-new car, something dies inside.

And that is probably what saved me from going off the deep end after a second animal went at my almost-brand-new car. Once you've got cat scratches, antler gouges and hoof prints sort of fit right in.

Tomatoes

My story, like lots of guys' stories, is about getting involved with a beautiful tomato. I'm not talking about infatuation or lust; I'm telling you I was ready to kill. Before it was over, I felt humiliation and guilt and the censure of my family. The beautiful tomato couldn't have cared less.

To return to the beginning, it was spring, a particularly sultry day in May, and I gambled on doing some planting ahead of time. In the ground I put many favorites: bell peppers, eggplants, the parsley and basil, and the most glorious plants of all, my Big Girl tomatoes. The gamble with the weather paid off. It remained warm right through Memorial Day. The crops were on their way. I was hoping to harvest the best Big Girl tomatoes ever in a decade of backyard farming.

Then he came along. At first, I tried to ignore him. But I noticed his burrow was getting bigger, more and more bold. My three small children and I began spotting him in the early morning and near dusk. They liked him, but he began to fill me with a sense of concern that would soon turn to loathing.

The woodchuck went after our favorite annuals. I'd planted row after row of the big cut-and-come-again zinnias, Evelyn's favorites. But on the calmest mornings following the most serene nights, I began to find my early flowers and even whole stems snapped off.

We returned home late on day to find Megan the cat, a sweet American domestic short hair, badly battered, a diagonal slash across her nose and a bald spot on her left hind leg where the fur had been ripped off. The children cuddled and caressed her as I tried to place balm over her wounds. We wondered which neighborhood dog had beaten her up. In the middle of the night it came to me: It was no dog. Megan had poked her curious puss into the woodchuck's hole and caught a flashing claw across the face. Then, as she tried to escape, the woodchuck had leaped up and let her have it across the leg.

All this time, the tomatoes and other edible plants seemed to thrive. Aware that fertilizer too soon produces great leaves but small fruit, I refrained. Pert yellow tomato blossoms appeared. I remained unrelenting in my weeding and dusting for insects, and I started picking off the sucker leaves. Promising green fruits began to appear.

A few years earlier, when two woodchucks lived off my land, I succumbed to dropping a few heavily thorned branches into their holes, with some mothballs for good measure. They seemed to depart and the children, asking wide-eyed where the woodchucks had gone, had made me feel beastly. Which is why this time I held off. I sensed the animal would not be satisfied with the zinnias alone but hoped he would not molest my Big Girl tomatoes. It was a dopey hope. One morning I found a few green tomatoes on the ground, a bite out of each.

The season grew hotter. Knowing my tomatoes would be nearly ripe and perfect by late July, I stepped up visits to that area of the garden. A strange and unsettling phenomenon was occurring: Not one tomato seemed to be reaching maturity. Oddly, I didn't catch on at first and kept feeding them water and fertilizer. Then it hit me like a ton of peat moss.

"Get one of those traps that doesn't hurt the animal," I urged Evelyn. A friend from the state's upper reaches said, "Don't even think of it. There's nothing more ornery than a trapped woodchuck. Exactly what do you think you're going to do with him once he's inside the cage?"

Good question. Then I dialed the nursery for help. By this time it was August and I'd yet to sample one luscious homegrown tomato. "Here's what you do," said the nurseryman. "Get a wheelbarrow full of stones and soil. Obtain a road flare. Fill one end of the burrow, light the flare and drop it in the other end and fill up the second hole. Presto! If your woodchuck's at home, it's execution and burial in one simple action."

I had to mull that one. I tried the idea on Evelyn. She shuddered. I mentioned the suggestion to the children. They stared at me as though I were a monster.

Weeks slipped by. The tomato plants looked increasingly ragged. My frustration grew. One Saturday afternoon when no one else was home, I jumped into the car, bought a package of flares at the auto supply shop, rushed home, and ... did nothing.

A few days later, I returned to the garden and after a thorough search could locate only one somewhat ripe Big Girl. I twisted it off, placed it in the kitchen window and went for the flares and the wheelbarrow. By the time the children returned home I was feeling strange, something akin, I imagine, to a soldier after his first brush with death on the battlefield. I told the children—confessed is a better word—and they seemed confused, if not bewildered. They said very little.

I went back to the gravesite several times, wondering how long it had taken for the flare to smoke the woodchuck into oblivion. The tomatoes, except for the one little beauty I'd rescued, were ruined for the season. But at least their destroyer was gone too.

Arriving back from a trip to the city the next day, I was told that our boy Charles had something to tell me and that he'd recorded it in a journal he keeps. I was busy, but Evelyn persisted. I opened the journal and read and couldn't believe my eyes.

"The woodchuck dug his way out after Dad buried him." I raced down to the spot. There was a fresh mound of dirt and two large stones, one of them scorned from the burning flare.

Well, I assured myself, he must have been the most scared woodchuck in creation; we won't be seeing him again. How he survived the fumes and had found the strength and cunning to uncover the tunnel from inside, I couldn't begin to fathom.

I remembered the one beautiful, if not fully developed, Big Girl that symbolized all this anguish and violence and went inside to savor it. It wasn't beautiful anymore; its skin was marred by spots of black mold. Ruefully, I tossed it out. I'd made a fool of myself. And the ostracizing was not yet complete. A few days later, the three children came running in shouting, "Daddy, Daddy, he's back!"

That's my story. Would I do the same dumb thing again? I don't know. They say that when it comes to a beautiful tomato you never learn your lesson. But right now I've got the seed catalogue open to the page on pole beans.

Vandals

One hot summer night not long ago, there was a sudden racket at the window near my pillow. I leaped from the bed and grabbed a petrified stick I keep behind the door. "Who is it? What do you want? Get out of here!" I shouted. My wife awakened, startled. There was no answer from the outside, just the same strange noise. I found a flashlight with my free hand and threw its beam at the window, ready to fight. A huge moth continued to beat its wings against the screen.

The incident made a dramatic point. After five years in our dream house in the woods, I remained afraid of it. Maybe it was because of the surroundings, which are beautiful, or because of the absence of neighbors, which in my waking hours I deem a large blessing. Or maybe it was because of the two men who paid the house a visit one afternoon shortly after we'd moved in when no one was there.

They carefully sliced back a screen, lifted an open dining room window, stepped in, removed a television set and a jewelry box and departed by the same window.

My poor wife delivered the news by telephone. My reaction was childish, or maybe childlike. It was as if someone bent on malice had kicked over a lovingly created sand castle. "So much for paradise," I told Evelyn.

The police came and determined a most curious thing. The alarm system, which is supposed to phone and send them scurrying to our address, guns drawn, to trap the interlopers, didn't go off because the wires in the cellar had been snipped. "You're new here, aren't you? Just had new phones installed?" the officer asked. "Well, the phone people, they spotted a line they didn't recognize. They should have asked you about it, but they cut it instead."

I was by then too concerned about my wife and our three little children to vent my outrage at the phone man. Despite our whispered conversations and outward nonchalance, the children sensed our true feelings—anger and disappointment and, most of all, sadness—and became afraid to play outdoors. Bit by bit, like youngsters testing the water and tide, they returned, but it took months.

We had the alarm reattached, and I told the insurance man about the crime. "You have a choice: sue the phone company or we'll simply honor your claim; it's up to you." A check came in the mail.

Replacing the television set was easy; the jewelry not so, particularly the small, old-fashioned diamond ring. It had been slipped onto my wife's finger by my mother on their second meeting, before our marriage. It had been my mother's quiet, generous way of welcoming Evelyn into our family. It had been my mother's persuasive method of telling me to grab Evelyn before she got away.

Not long after the break-in, I attended a local P.T.A. lecture on teaching children to be wary of strangers. When it was over, the police detective who had given the talk came up. "We got your men, arrested them over in Larchmont with a TV and jewelry box on the back seat, exact same M.O." He saw my eyes asking about our small heirlooms. "They admitted your job, but the stuff's gone. We're going to prosecute on the other job; we got a stronger case against them."

It was reassuring to learn the crooks would not be back. But since that time, to my chagrin, the alert police have appeared in my driveway (guns holstered) on a few occasions because the alarm works very well indeed. The last time, I was entrapped by my wife, who insisted she would not activate the alarm system before departing. The moment I opened the door, the jig was up.

One July Fourth weekend, hooligans climbed a tree near the road on my property and cut down and swiped our American flag. I was not scared that they would become more daring and try to enter the house, but the indecency of their act was flabbergasting.

And this past July Fourth, a new flag flying, I tossed most of the night as firecrackers burst up and down the road. I imagined the new flag gone and the mailbox being blown up, as had already happened to three other mailboxes nearby. Bleary at dawn, I padded down the long driveway and was renewed to find all intact.

A recent night, however, brought epiphany. At two o'clock or so, the photoelectric cell of the alarm system began clicking. The sound, meant to detect menace, was in the middle of the night menacing itself. I listened without moving from bed. The sound stopped for a while and then resumed. It became accompanied by the noises of moving around, bumping against pipes and beams, brushing against boxes and shelves. Something serious was going on in the cellar.

This time I did not reach for my petrified stick or a flashlight or even the telephone. I was pleased to discover that a lot of the old fear was not there. Evelyn had left open several casement windows, which would permit someone or something to enter the house. But, I reckoned, the doors were all locked, including the one leading up from the cellar. The noises and clicking went on for thirty or sixty minutes, and then I heard a scampering through the woods. It wasn't the first time we had had this visitor.

In the morning, I entered the cellar and found a box of canning wax opened and chewed and some paper plates and plastic cups knocked about. The raccoon had returned, found our hospitality wanting and stomped off.

I wish he had waited. I would have told him not to be afraid of me, just as I had become unafraid of him. I would have told him, "Thank you." I would have let him know my house is finally starting to feel like home.

Squirrels

I'd like to meet the inventor of the squirrel-proof bird feeder. I'd like to tell him he's nuts. Of course, if he (or she) made a minor adjustment in the name of the invention, I wouldn't have a kernel of a complaint. Call it what it is: the bird-proof squirrel feeder.

I'm talking about our redwood, house-shaped feeder with the glass panels, front and back porch, and the large, curved upside-down dish arranged over it. This dish is supposed to send squirrels and all other proponents of the free lunch sliding off and nose-diving to the ground. The dish is called a baffle; it shows the inventor at least had a sense of humor.

But talk, as the bird lovers at my house have found out, is "cheep." The feeder is delicately nestled among clump birches and a variety of evergreen bushes. All the experts say you have to provide protection for your birds, give them the serenity of cover when they come to feed. And the birds do come often, but it does them very little good because chances are the squirrels are dining. Sometimes there are so many I've thought of installing one of those devices you find at the delicatessen counter with the sign, "Take a number even when we're not busy." While one squirrel shimmies down from the squirrel-proof baffle, others wait on the birch branches or in the rhododendron for their turn. I'll give them this much: they are very polite to each other.

But they are devastating to the birds and bird lovers. The feeder was set up outside our kitchen window, both so we could enjoy the wintering birds and so we would know when it was time to refill the little redwood house with their favorite seed. We became so fond of the birds—not just the tufted titmice, chickadees, and nuthatches but even the blue jays—that we purchased gourmet seed with the slogan on the bag, "The Best That Money Can Buy."

Squirrels have got to be into networking. It's the only way I can explain it. One must have discovered our Zabar's In the Woods and bragged to another and on and on, by word of mouth, until they began lining up most mornings. I could even swear they had smiles on their faces. The birds were getting to eat only when the squirrels were so sated that they'd lumbered off for a snooze in some local tree hollows.

My instincts told me the way to deal with the problem was not to get mad at nature but to cooperate with it, to use the sense and rhythms of nature and understand its harmony. I tried that. Squirrels are rodents, cats detest rodents, so I ordered Megan the cat—stalker and retriever of mice, chipmunks, birds, and even rabbits—off our newly recovered living room couch and out into nature. She was back in a few minutes, eager to return to the task of protecting the couch. Not only had she failed to catch a squirrel, she hadn't even intimidated one.

We humans took to tapping on the window. It seemed to distract and annoy the squirrels for a while, but I feared enthusiastic tapping was leading to banging, and banging might lead to smashed windows and sliced hands and problems even bigger than bird-proof squirrel feeders.

So we set up an alert. When my wife or I or one of the three children spotted a squirrel doing its acrobatic gourmandizing, we'd rush outdoors and commence harrowing screams. It worked! It worked beautifully except for one flaw: to make it truly effective, I'd have to resign my job, my wife would have to be quarantined to the kitchen, and the children would have to drop out of school.

But, I asked myself, why continue to wallow in amateurism? I went to an expert at a nearby nursery. He listened patiently and then reached for what looked like a tube of caulking compound with a long plastic nozzle. "Use it sparingly," he said, "it works every time. They even use it to keep the squirrels off the telephone lines." I peered around his shop and noticed all the bird feeders and the squirrel-proof baffles, but in my excitement it didn't occur to ask why he was selling the compound if he believed in the baffles. The stuff turned out to be a particularly egregious type of axle grease. I was hours trying to get traces of it off my hands, but I had the squirrel-proof baffle dish lathered with it and sat back to wait for the satisfying—and, I figured, hilarious—results.

It was funny all right. The next morning, with my family gathered at the window, the platoon of squirrels showed up. As usual, the first leaped from a birch branch and onto the chain from which the feeder is hung, began to make his way to the feeder itself, and leaped onto the baffle. "Watch this, folks, this is going to be great," I chortled. The squirrel, as was his habit, simply shimmied down the baffle, hung upside down over the feeder and began breakfast.

I couldn't believe it. Instead of sliding unceremoniously into the void, little rodent legs flailing desperately, hitting the hard ground with a wallop and networking the experience to all his buddies, he was managing to hold on with no apparent trouble at all.

It's been months since this drama began, but we've finally achieved a harmony with nature and I guess that's the lesson in this whole tale. Every morning early one of us goes out and screams and rants for a minute, which clears the area of squirrels. The titmice and their friends dine for a while, and then the squirrels return for their share. But meanwhile I say we yank the patent on the squirrel-proof bird feeder, and while we're at it, yank the foolproof squirrel grease, too.

Fighting Battles

Mrs. Ferguson threw me out of her house. She didn't pick me up and toss me across the stoop and onto the grass, though I'm sure a person her size would have been capable of it. Instead she blocked the doorway and said I would not be permitted to read the *Times* in her parlor while my daughter took a piano lesson.

"Mrs. Ferguson," I said, "I find this strange. I find it insulting. What am I supposed to do for thirty minutes in the cold?"

"You could go to the market," she said. As we sparred, Sara with her books slipped beneath us into the music room.

"Mrs. Ferguson, there is no market. You live across from a cemetery."

"I know, I know," she said, her brown eyes now bright with anger and defiance.

"There'll be no lesson for my daughter where there's no respect for her father!" I wanted to shout, but instead I spun around to avoid seeing the door shut in my face, returned to the car and waited. As much as I was tempted, I would not use my little girl to fight my battles.

The exchange had the quality of ritual. I already knew that I was not welcome. Mrs. Ferguson had told my wife that her husband needed the parlor. I had met Mr. Ferguson, a silent, good-looking, gray-haired misanthrope who hid his incivility behind the excuse of poor health. He seemed to spend his days alternately dozing and staring at the newspaper. I suspected the main reason I was ejected was not Mr. Ferguson but Mrs. Ferguson, who would not risk my listening and judging her performance as a teacher. I suspected also that beneath her apparent patience with Sara and the trappings of kindness, like the candy jar on her piano, was a capacity for cruelness.

A half-hour later Sara appeared at the car. I kept my face in the Op-Ed page and handed her seven dollars, which she carried back to the house. "Bye-bye, Sara, see you next week," said the kindly sounding voice from the door.

"How'd she treat you?" I asked my daughter.

"Okay," she said.

"You tell her I'd like to get rid of her?"

"You always ask me that, Daddy. I didn't tell her."

I should mention that Mrs. Ferguson is a criminal. For her services, she demanded payment in cash, as do, I imagine, Mafia killers and Colombian cocaine kingpins. I had considered alerting the Internal Revenue Service and collecting a bounty, but when I floated the idea past my wife Evelyn, who is Irish, her blue eyes flashed, and she went extremely Irish on me.

The song arrived in warm weather, in the summer, as if on a breeze that drifted through the bushes, found its way through the casement window and wafted into the kitchen. But instead of providing only a moment's refreshment, it lingered, teased us, insinuated itself, grew stronger, and by its beauty began to haunt us.

Sara tried to pick it out on the piano, but it was elusive, like trying to find the right words to describe a special sunset at a pond near the sea in Maine or a woman's profile that appeared momentarily between the arms, shoulders, hats and newspapers of other passengers on a crowded bus on your first visit to Manhattan.

No one could quite remember where the song came from, whether on the radio or television or phonograph record or tape. We played our collection for several days, hoping to find the song. We then decided that someone must have hummed or whistled it. All of us, parents, Sara, and her two brothers, took up humming, though it was often difficult to believe we all were attempting the same melody.

The song joined the household, just as surely as Megan the cat had joined us four years earlier, and our wish to identify it took hold and hung on for many days.

"Listen to this, Sara," I might say. "I think I've got it. Da-da, da-da, da-da, da-da, daa …"

"No, it goes daa-da, daa-da, daa-da, daaaa …"

We drove to a shopping mall and found a music store called Rock Heaven. As we stood at the entrance, Sara stared at me with a look of amusement one would expect to see on the face of a sassy, grown-up woman. "We're going in anyhow," I said.

The young clerk had spiked hair with a miniature pigtail at the neck, a gold earring, a skinny black tie and trousers like the bottom half of a George Raft zoot suit. "We're looking for some sheet music …"

"Don't have sheet music," he interrupted, "only tapes, compact discs, electric guitars and accessories."

"Fine, we're also looking for a tape."

"Give me the artist and name of album."

"Well, you see, we don't really know. We don't care who the artist is. We're simply hoping to get a tape of the music."

He seemed put-upon but asked the name of the song. I was hoping Sara would pick up the conversation, but all she did was look at me with that face.

"Da-da, da-da, da-da, da-da, daa …" I said.

"What?" he exclaimed.

I repeated it even louder, with the abandon that comes of hopelessness. The clerk stomped off.

On another day we spotted a music shop in town near our home and drove by it several times, like robbers sizing up a prospective heist. All we could see through the windows were blue-and-red speckled guitars and a drum set, and we decided to pass it up.

The search became especially tantalizing because Sara's eighth birthday was a week away. What better gift to present her with than the beautiful song? At night Evelyn and I decided we would work overtime to identify the music. The next morning, feeling like investigators showing around snapshots of a missing person, we began humming the song to people we met. Many claimed to know the song and expressed fondness for it; no one knew its name.

Three days before Sara's birthday, it occurred to me we had overlooked an important source. "I can't call her, Evelyn. She threw me out of her house, remember?"

I paced the living room as Evelyn telephoned Mrs. Ferguson. No one was home, but several tries later I heard Evelyn hum the song and explain its importance.

"Well?" I asked when she hung up.

"She says it's too hard for Sara. She'll begin to teach it to her in the fall."

"Are you not moved by the way our girl goes to the piano day after day, trying to capture that song? Do you think she ought to wait two months?"

"She says Sara will learn it wrong, the wrong fingering and so forth, unless she's there to teach it."

"We don't need her," I concluded brusquely. "What does she know about children, anyway? I'm the father and I say she can learn the song immediately. What's it called?"

Evelyn's voice sank to the level of a whisper that one might use while watching the sputtering fuss of a large firecracker. "Mrs. Ferguson wouldn't tell me," she said.

The ticking clock made me desperate. I called people I hadn't spoken to in months. "Da-da, da-da, da-da, da-da, daaa ... well, thanks anyway." Two nights before the birthday, I found myself humming the song in the company of a friend. "That's so pretty," she said lightly, "'Für Elise' by Beethoven."

"Are you kidding?"

"Why, no," she said, startled by my excitement. "It may be the only classical piece I know by name, but that's it."

Evelyn was on the phone the next morning, and by ten o'clock had located a music store that had not only the sheet music but three versions of it. I canceled all previous plans and drove to the city, anxiously picturing a scene in which the very last copy of the music is being sold and slipped into an envelope just as I rush in. At the store, a man at the front sent me to the proper department, where another man called for a woman who pulled open a file draw and reached in to fulfill the request.

I can't read music, but I ran my eyes across the first page, humming a few notes here and there, making believe I was deciding whether this was the best score for my needs. My humming must have been awful, for the young woman said finally, "That's the simplest one we have." The price was $2.95. I thanked her and marveled at such a small sum for such a great prize.

The store carried no recorded music but directed me to a large record and tape store several blocks away, where a clerk accompanied me to the classical department, found Beethoven and the sub-category of piano music, and helped me search—to no avail. She called for a man who seemed to be an assistant manager and, from appearance, something of a longhair.

He looked briefly through the same racks of tapes. "Look, I have an idea," he said. "Do you have a favorite classical music radio station? Call them and ask for the program director and sing him the melody and say you must locate 'Für Elise' and I'm sure if you're polite and he's not too busy he'll help you." He and the woman clerk left me to glumly imagine the outcome of such an impractical if not outright ludicrous suggestion.

On the way out of the classical department, I spied one more section of tapes—the cheap ones by lesser known orchestras and artists. I went through every row and was down to the last half-dozen when I was granted a religious experience. "Für Elise" read the sleeve. It was the opening piece of a selection called "Romantic Piano Music." The pianist was Wilhelm Kempff. I raced to the counter and told the serious assistant manager, "I found it! It's absolutely amazing!" He seemed pleased for me and examined the case. "Deutsche Grammophon, a very good label," he said. It was the second miracle in an hour and had cost only $3.99.

The next day Evelyn and I presented to Sara, among other gifts, the sheet music and tape. She was pleased but not ecstatic, went to the piano and tentatively clunked out the first several bars of the song. Then she played the tape. How lovely it was.

A few days later, hearing the sounds—da-da, da-da, da-da, daa, da-da-daaa, da-da, daaa—wafting out the same window that seemed to have brought it to us in the first place, I ran inside. "Is it Kempff or cutie pie?" I shouted. There she was, standing at the piano in her pink sneakers, gazing up at the sheet music, flawlessly performing "Für Elise."

"It was cutie pie," she said after she'd finished.

Evelyn and I and the boys congratulated her. She was pleased but refrained from her standard bow, one palm of the hand in the small of the back, the other across the waist. She seemed to be acknowledging that Beethoven had something to do with her accomplishment.

"I told you that Mrs. Ferguson was all wet …" I began to hiss to Evelyn. "Not now, dear," she replied. "Sara, would you favor us one more time?"

With the end of summer and the start of school we returned to the house across from the cemetery. I made sure Sara brought the "Für Elise" sheet music to play for her doubting mentor. I paced outside, sizing up suitable tombstones for the gracious couple, imagining the delicious moment when Sara stepped to the keyboard and produced her beautiful song.

Thirty minutes later she scampered out, as she always did, with the kindly sounding voice behind her singing, "See you next week." By then I'd become almost too excited to read the duller opinion-makers on the Op-Ed page.

When Sara was in the car I asked, "How'd you make out, my little darling?"

"She said I didn't do it right. She said she'd have to teach me the right way. Then we played other songs out of the regular book."

I felt a swell of emotion and the blood rushed to my head. I stared through the windshield, and after a long time asked, "What shall we do? We can come back while we seek a new teacher or we can drive away and never come back."

"You always ask that," she said.

"Oh, Sara, I'm so sorry. You weren't supposed to fight my battles."

When our gazes met I was looking into other eyes, grown-up and wise. "It's okay, Daddy," she told me. "I didn't mind."

Virtuosity

When I was twenty years old, I bought a piano for twenty dollars and had it moved into the small living room of the apartment I shared with my parents, brother, and sister. This action was taken without anyone's encouragement and with considerable consternation from my mother. I did not know how to play the piano, did not have a piano teacher, and had demonstrated no musical promise beyond the stamina in high school to beat a snare drum more or less as instructed in the marching band. The piano actually had cost nothing; the twenty dollars went to three strong movers wearing denim aprons. The one who was white seemed to be the boss, though the work was distributed democratically. They drove the large, black, oblong monster to our building from an owner thrilled to be rid of it and hefted it up the steep front stairs and then up another stairway to the second floor. I tipped them two dollars, which was all I had left, and wondered later how they would divide it.

I began to play immediately. I pecked out tunes with the forefinger of my right hand. Unlike Irving Berlin, who played only black notes, I relied on the white notes, always starting at middle C. Middle C was my musical home, a place to venture forth from and a place to return to as often as possible, like a small bird flying by tentative daring instead of carefree intuition. Sometimes the white notes failed me; they just could not produce the sound I sought, and it was only then that I ventured a half-note up or down, often alighting onto the mysterious black keys. After several right-hand pecking sessions, I became really bold and began to play with both hands. My method was to strike with the middle finger of the left hand the same note, two octaves lower, that the right was playing, with the thumb and baby finger splayed in such a way as to constitute a chord.

At the other end of the apartment, my mother listened to these golden days of musical discovery, I was certain, but she rarely entered the room during my performances and never commented on them. When she stared at the piano, a forlorn look came over her.

After three or four weeks of persistence my repertoire included "September Song," "Night and Day," "I'm in the Mood for Love," "They Can't Take That Away from Me" and, for reasons beyond my own comprehension, "The Volga Boatman." When it became apparent I was not going to give up the piano but might play my simple versions of these songs into eternity—I remember being hurt when a visitor laughed at my skill and called it "cocktail lounge music"—my mother sought divine intervention. She called the rabbi's wife.

I had vaguely considered lessons, putting the subject aside because I was already enjoying myself and had no extra money for a music teacher, but the rabbi's wife prevailed. She arranged for me to meet a woman she claimed had been a concert pianist in Europe and who had studied with the great Schnabel—a name I thought was for a dog but later realized was important. I took the streetcar to meet the teacher.

She was a small woman, rather like a large midget, and she immediately ushered me into her music room, leaped up onto her piano bench, and started to play immensely complicated and sometimes beautiful music. She then beckoned me to sit next to her and held her hand up to mine. "See, your hand is bigger than mine. I have trouble playing even one complete octave. You will be able to stretch beyond an octave." This statement was delivered in some comical Middle European accent and was intended to make a profound impression, but rubbing hands with this strange woman only frightened me, and I wanted to go as soon as possible. But she reached up and flipped a page above the keyboard. "Do you read? No? I will teach you to read. You will love it. It is a whole new language," she said, and resumed playing.

This time, she became entranced by her music and began to sway back and forth. I felt like the member of the trapeze family who moves to and fro on the floor of the Big Top while the star completes the amazing trick overhead. It made me almost sick to think of catching this creature in my arms. But her balance was expert, and she completed the piece and asked if I had liked it. I nodded, and she quickly turned a page and launched into a new song, this one even more dramatic than the last. It soon became clear she had forgotten I was sitting only a foot from her, for she became excited by the music and began to pant. When she sucked for extra air, she pulled her lips back to reveal large, straight teeth and her nostrils flared and her head rolled, and I was both repulsed and spellbound by this woman who had turned herself into a musical horse.

"Did you like that?" she said, when she had returned to normal. "It was very beautiful, and we will make that your first project." The name of the music and the composer I never really grasped. But she had me in her thrall, and my diligent study of the piano commenced.

The piece was beautiful, and I learned it well, though the student of the student of the great Schnabel developed a habit of composing—improving the music, so to speak, making it his own, adding humorous trills or somber bass chords, or playful staccatos borrowed from drum-roll days—much to the displeasure of the teacher. As a result, I learned two major pieces of music those days after the long streetcar ride, that of the great Mendelssohn, or whatever his name was, and that of my own composition. But the only time she ever registered actual disgust was when, half way through the eloquent melody, she suddenly heard "Night and Day."

Aside from what she called my "American lack of discipline," the teacher was impressed. Maybe even Schnabel might have been impressed. My mother wasn't impressed. She had not had much exposure to the "the classics," as I had begun to call my playing, and she found my interpretations of popular songs too rinky-dink for her romantic tastes.

Yet one day she announced a great new interest in the piano. As it turned out, her enthusiasm was not for the music but for its appearance. She set out to turn the piano into what she called "an antique." For several days, she worked happily and long, applying a series of special paints until the black hulk was gone, and in its place a large, graceful instrument with an attractive cream-colored finish, flecked with strokes of gold. Everyone in the family complimented her.

"Where is it, Ma?" I asked, still beyond shock, upon climbing the stairs and entering the living room one afternoon less than a week later. We stared together at the once-again empty wall. Her hands were folded at the waist over her apron. "Oh, it looked so beautiful, a dozen wanted it," she said. "One outbid the other. They begged me for it. What could I do?"

My Mother

A curious sound attracted me as I strolled one midday in Manhattan, and turning the corner I discovered a small crowd facing three young musicians earnestly playing violin, cornet, and clarinet. Some in the crowd smiled and others bobbed their heads from side to side in time to the music. The scene was incongruous. For one, the musicians were playing Klezmer music, the light yet melancholy and insistent melodies of a Jewish Europe that exists now only in sentiment and literature, but the same sounds that still can transform the most righteous males of the chosen into whirling dervishes. For another, the musicians—two men and a woman, who had the violin—stood in front of a dilapidated but stately Protestant church.

Shops and restaurants, buildings of a great university, towers of commerce loomed all around. But had a man just awakened from a sleep on a nearby bench, his eyes peering down at the ancient brick and paving stones of the square, the Klezmer music dancing into his ears, he might have believed he was in the ghetto of Cracow, Budapest, or Prague.

I found an inconspicuous spot under a weary plane tree, its bark gone to camouflage against the city blight, and marveled at the variety of people drawn to the concert. There were elderly widows and widowers, who paid each other absolutely no attention; two sturdy young men with expensive bicycles; a couple wearing denim pants and vests, both exposing tattoos of endearment; businessmen and ladies; men pale and dark in the causal paralysis of liquor or drugs or both.

One of the musicians, a thin, ungainly man aspiring for style under a Panama hat, preceded each number with a short tale about the song, its title and its place in Klezmer history. The truth was they all sounded pretty much the same; one might call it deedle-deedle-dee music. It is the kind of music that bands hired for lavish bar mitzvahs and weddings attempt every now and then between sets of cautious rock or ballads and cha-chas, the music that inspires a smile and a sigh and a turn of heads toward the old-timers.

Yet Klezmer music is more than that. It has a way of insinuating itself into your feelings, establishing a mystery while withholding the solution, demanding you accord it serious attention like the regard you would give a loved and honored relative. Standing there, I became mesmerized, yet aware of my almost perfect stillness, and the Klezmer delivered another incongruity. It transported me to an orchestra seat at the revival of *42nd Street*. I had purchased expensive tickets as a treat for my wife and me. The threadbare plot of the out-of-town girl who gets her big break and sings and dances her way to stardom left most of the audience amused and content. But for most of the show, I was in the clutches of strange and uninvited emotions. When the house lights were turned on, I made my way from the theater wet-faced and embarrassed. I had cried through most of the show. All I had really seen on that stage was my mother.

My mother might have been a star. She was a wonderful singer, dancer, and comedian. She could demand you fall in love with her when she sang, "One of These Days," and when you were hooked she would grin and dance, not a great dance but one with grace and humor. Then she would glide into "My Sweet Little Alice Blue Gown," and only a hardened criminal or unfortunate deaf man could fail to be touched. My mother could have stepped onto any center stage on Broadway or bowed to a black-tie and gown audience at Carnegie Hall and left them, an hour and a half later, exhausted from laughter and tears. The closest she got to Broadway was a hundred blocks away, behind the counter of a children's wear shop she operated with my father before he decided to move our young family up to Massachusetts. Her show business career began and ended in her living room.

Now, under the sun, watching the Klezmer clarinetist pump one foot as he played—for Klezmer without stomping is not Klezmer—I filled up suddenly with what I can only describe as an umbilical feeling, a yearning, unattainable as it was, for the career my mother never had. My thoughts shot back to a recent reunion. Seeing my wife and family and me made my elderly mother happy, and she began to sing. I know old people sing; it is their way of reviewing parts of their lives, placing the memories. But when my mother sang, she was not reliving the past so much as polishing up her repertoire. She knew she had an appreciative audience. Her singing gave us all satisfaction, including my father, for while her volume was gone, she still had the personality to bowl you over with a song. And when she sang, she forgot for a while her whole catalogue of hurts.

The Klezmer players finished a break, announced where next they would play, and with the lift of a foot and a nod of the Panama hat launched into their finale. I listened and wished I could grasp the hand of one of my children. A man who had been standing nearby, older than I and dressed well but casually, looked into my face. "What's the matter, young man? This is supposed to be happy music," he said kindly.

"I'm crying for my mother," I told him without shame. He nodded solemnly, stepped away to give me a measure of solitude and turned his attention back to the Klezmer musicians. "Deedle-deedle-dee," said the clarinet, sliding away from the bleat of the cornet and rising above the sweet rasp of the violin. "Deedle-deedle-dee, deedle-deedle-da."

Journey through the
Land of the Gaels

I was small and wretched, all the more so for being attached to the strong left hand of my noble mother as she rapped at the curtained glass door of our Dorchester neighbor. A tall, sullen man opened up. "Your son is twice the size of mine," said my mother. "Why did he and his hoodlums want to beat up my boy?" The man turned angry but remained silent. My mother pinched me hard on the arm. "Look. Doesn't it hurt? Don't you think we cry? Don't you think we bleed? Be our friend or leave us alone," she said.

As she spun us off the porch and back down the street, my mother whispered, "You have my permission. Next time his lug of a son bothers you, grab a board, a stone, anything, and let him have it." Thus was my introduction to Jewish-Irish relations in the city of Boston in the peace-loving years following World War II. But this experience did nothing to explain what I recognized, even as a small boy, as the love between my mother and Mrs. Courtney, the older Irish lady who lived in the house behind our triple-decker. They both seemed to glow when they met, embracing, talking animatedly, offering to shop for each other, cook, and bake. On her parlor wall, Mrs. Courtney hung framed slogans, embroidered in English and Gaelic, on the sanctity of the Irish and the family. One of her bachelor sons taught me to say "Kiss my butt" in Gaelic, but I could think of no one to say it to without the direst of consequences and soon forgot how.

One time I arrived home with a dollar bill tucked into the breast pocket of my High Holy Days jacket. "Mrs. Courtney said, 'Happy New Year, Little Darling,'" I told my mother, who burst into tears. Nor was the toughness of the streets in accord with the adoration that I sensed flowed between the couple next door I knew as Tom and Mary.

I could not forget the smiles and caresses of the hands and stolen pecks on the cheek that Tom and Mary bestowed on each other. They seemed to have boundless gentleness and desire for each other, and they became even then the romantic ideal to which I would aspire decades later.

But neither Tom and Mary nor Mrs. Courtney and her houseful of sons, all of whom seemed to work for the city, could make the streets safe. We were one of a handful of Jewish families in an overwhelmingly Irish neighborhood. It made no difference that my name was Arab. It wasn't Irish. I didn't look Irish, and I never showed up at St. Matthew's Church.

When my pious father enrolled me in a Hebrew school about a mile away, my mother had a new worry. "Don't wear your yarmulke on the street," she warned. "They'll kill you." And indeed, one afternoon shortly after I began religious studies, the local gang, a group of Irish kids led by the slight but cruel-tongued Jerry O'Hara, waited for my arrival at the corner of Woodrow Avenue and Wollaston Terrace. The barbarians moved in for some sport but suddenly stopped as if stricken and pointed to the top of my head. "Take that thing off and fight fair!" yelled O'Hara. They were afraid to strike a holy man, or at least a holy boy. I got very used to wearing my yarmulke.

I had a gentile friend, Roberto Francesco Grande, now a Boston artist, who lived near Franklin Park and did not look Irish. An Irish gang chased him down Seaver Street, screaming anti-Semitic epithets into his Mediterranean ears, trapped him in the park, and tied him to a tree. Another time, they waited in ambush, preparing to pelt him with trolley-track stones. "I ran too fast, the stones never touched me," Grande said. I was not so fortunate. Early one evening, as I was walking on Oakhurst Street, a stone flew into my left cheek. The doctor opened his office on Norfolk Street and sewed up my face. The worst part was looking at the scar every day until it faded away twenty years later.

When I was a teenager, my mother delivered a new lecture one afternoon in our kitchen. "Don't get mixed up with an Irish girl. They're cute as a button. They'll bill and coo. But the first time you have a fight," she said, becoming agitated, "the Irish girl will scream, 'You Dirty Jew!'" How could my mother know this? True, she suffered the immigrant's plight of seeming to need another group to knock, but she was given to abundant kindness as well. Irish girls were definitely cute. I loved watching them at City Point Beach in South Boston, their lips purple and fair skin covered with goose bumps as they emerged from the cold water. They didn't seem to have boyfriends, only large numbers of tall brothers, skinny like them. Northeastern University changed everything. It was not exactly the Dublin of the New World, but the campus offered an array of people I had scarcely known existed: Poles, Swedes, hardscrabble WASPs, French-Canadians, Italians, and Sicilians. And many Irish men and women. Did it occur to us then that we were almost all the same—bright, ambitious, wanting to feel grown-up and have a little forbidden fun, most of all hoping to lift ourselves solidly into the middle class? I don't think so. I carried my disastrous and comical self-consciousness toward all women with me at all times, feigning comfort only in large noisy groups at lunch or in the quadrangle.

But another kind of miracle occurred. I began to develop friendships with Irish men. They wanted to talk, share jokes, discuss why a professor was unduly severe, whether I liked best the brunette from Swampscott, the blonde from Wrentham, or the Chinese girl from the South End. In the classrooms, I began to see the Irish beyond the pug-nosed tormentors and their untouchable sisters. I learned of the devastating famine of the nineteenth century, The Troubles in the fight for independence, the abuse suffered by Irish immigrants to Boston and other parts of America. I began to appreciate the superb Irish literary legacy of Joyce and Yeats. This discovery of the possibilities and richness of Irish people took another great leap shortly after my arrival at the *Boston Globe* to begin my chores as a copyboy. Most of the senior editors were Yankee Protestants, but the majority of the reporters were Irishmen. I found them determined, sentimental, funny, boisterous, kind, and honorable. After a couple of weeks on the job, I wanted nothing so much in the world as to become a reporter just like them.

Late one Saturday, when the deadlines were past, three of the middle-aged reporters told me we were going out. We walked to a bar where they were known, near North Station, and as soon as we settled on our stools the bartender placed a shot of rye and a glass of beer—the perilous boilermaker—in front of each of us. I watched them throw down the whiskey and guzzle the beer, and I did the same. We did this three times, a different reporter pushing cash across the bar each time.

I also sensed they were watching to see if I'd slide off my stool. But I reached into my pocket and ordered a fourth round, and after we all drank, they smiled at one another and laughed and slapped me on the back. It was a strange ritual that left me reeling, but shortly afterward the three reporters and almost every other person in the City Room began to teach me how to be a reporter.

One other student and copyboy, in particular, offered his friendship and opened my eyes to the intricate and colorful world of the Boston Irish. Robert J. Anglin was a complex man who could be as sweet as Jerry O'Hara, the street-corner thug, had been feral. While O'Hara practiced animosity, Anglin took me home to meet his family, invited me to rented summer houses on Cape Cod, introduced me to his friends in taverns and restaurants across Dorchester and South Boston. He charmed bartenders, established tabs, argued Greek philosophy or Roman history, and fairly often threw punches. "Bob," I would say nervously as we approached one of our hangouts, "remember you're a lover, not a fighter." He fixed me up with an Irish girl. I pulled up to her house in Southie, vaguely expecting that in the next few moments I might be dragged from the car and left bloodied in the gutter. Instead a glorious-looking girl, reminiscent of a teenage Lauren Bacall, leaned out her window and waved and said she'd be right down. Bob's only counsel had been not to try anything too sexually exotic on the first date. I was delighted that he perceived me as, well, so romantically dangerous, but the truth was I'd had little experience of any kind. The Irish girl and I went through the motions of dinner and conversation, but the evening never came alive. I drove her home and dreamed about her for a long time.

Bob stayed at the *Globe* while I established a writing career in New York. Early one evening several years later, I stopped for a beer at the Kettle of Fish on MacDougal Street in Greenwich Village. As my eyes grew accustomed to the dimness, I could not believe what I saw. Sitting across the oak oval bar was Jerry O'Hara. I guess we humans are imbued with affection for old times, even unpleasant old times, because I waved to O'Hara, suggesting he join me and tell me why he was in town. By then I had completed the warrior phase of my life, having survived a series of professional prizefights, but even as Jerry ambled over, I felt an old and anxious chill. Seconds later, it was replaced by a rising fury, because as he pulled up the stool, Jerry was wearing his malicious smirk, like he used to on Woodrow Avenue. "Jerry," I said, "the way I see it, you have two choices here. One, you can buy me a beer and we can have a conversation. Two, we can go outside and I can give you the whipping of your life." Who knows what might have happened? He bought, we had an uneventful chat, and parted.

Evelyn, actually Mary Evelyn Rose—descended from the Gallaghers and Mulhearns, daughter of Counties Mayo and Roscommon—was beautiful, smart, and effervescent, and I was captivated by her. She worked for the president of a Manhattan public relations firm where I'd recently been hired. One day, when she was dropping off papers in my office, I reached for the kind of glibness that masked my inhibition and asked her to sit in my lap. We all know that commissions and courts can be convened, careers destroyed by such ideas. But much to my fascination, she planted herself exactly as I had proposed, smiled, and then jumped up. It led to nothing else. She refused to go out on a date, declaring that if the liaison went bad, it might make office life unbearable.

The president of the firm liked to have his troops leap up when he appeared or tremble in his presence. Knowing that, I stubbornly refused. I was doing good work and, besides, I had only recently outfoxed Jerry O'Hara. After I'd been there a few weeks, the president's chief aide arrived at my door one day. "I know it's crazy," he said, "but the boss says you're fired." I can't pretend I wasn't stunned. I'd never been fired, but the hurt was soon relieved. I found Evelyn. "I just got fired," I told her cheerfully. "I don't work here anymore. Now can we go out?"

"Yes," she said. Several months later, already knowing she was the Mary to my Tom, Evelyn and I drove to Boston. She had met some of my friends—Bob Anglin weighed in by saying she was too good for me—but I wanted her to meet my parents. I was certain that they would find her a young woman of rare and desirable qualities. I introduced her to them in the living room of their apartment in Hyde Park and then slipped with my mother into the kitchen for coffees and cake. "Well, Mom, how do you like her?" I asked. "She's lovely," said my mother. "Never bring her here again." It became a pivotal moment of my life. "Mom," I said, keeping calm, "you got that out of your

system. I hope to never hear you speak about Evelyn that way again."
She didn't reply.

The ambivalence toward Evelyn in Hyde Park was matched if not surpassed by that toward me in her household on Staten Island. Although her sisters spoke to me and seemed enthusiastic, I had by this time developed a built-in blarney-meter, and the dial was bouncing all over the place. Her mother expressed her unhappiness by remaining aloof and, when I was not present, desperately trying to convince her daughter she might be making the mistake of her life. Evelyn's father had died only months before we had become acquainted, and the mantle of patriarch had gone to her older brother, a well-educated, socially cautious man who let it be known he was not pleased by our relationship, leading me to believe he opposed us on religious grounds.

My mother meddled again. We were out for a Sunday ride during another visit to Boston, my dad at my side, Evelyn and my mom in the back seat. I suddenly noticed in the rearview mirror that my mother was fidgeting with her fingers. A few minutes later, the woman who had unwittingly invoked Shakespeare to protect her little boy in Dorchester completed another of her dramatic gestures and asked Evelyn to show us her left hand. I hadn't proposed or even contemplated the place and circumstances. It was too late. "Your girlfriend's wearing a diamond ring," said my mother, as Evelyn smiled demurely. "It looks like you two are engaged. Your father and I wish you a long and happy life." Which, thanks to God, it has been, due in no small measure to our children, Edward, Charles, and Sara.

But more than twenty years passed with scarcely a phone call between my house and that of Evelyn's brother John. While we had raised three children, he and his wife, Yvonne, had raised four. I pictured them as an eccentric and bitter family, draped in their sanctimony. I also had no way of measuring my wife's tribal loyalty to them. One night on vacation in Rockport, Massachusetts, we stayed too late and drank too much with good friends, the Jeremiah V. Murphy family. Murphy was a former *Globe* man, Pulitzer Prize winner, and onetime colleague. In my condition, the warmth and hospitality of the Murphys suddenly summoned memories of the opposite: painful, old feelings of rejection by my Irish kin.

Returning on foot to the nearby inn where our children slept, I began to itemize, even codify, the manifold inadequacies of Evelyn's small-minded family. She protested for a few blocks, then adjusted her strategy. It became known as The Night Evelyn Slugged Me on Granite Street. Yet there was an increasingly powerful desire to see them that I could not quite understand. And it was Evelyn who ultimately had the courage to call and insist that they jump into their van and drive the 150 miles to our home for a reunion. Arriving late for my own party with last-minute groceries, I entered the living room and everyone stopped talking. Their first-born, Heather, crossed the room, and threw her arms around me and we held each other for what seemed a long time. Her sister, Tara, offered a hug. Andrew and Brian, teenage boys, shook my hand. One of them called me "Uncle Herb." Uncle Herb. That sounded good. These children could not have been told that I was some disagreeable philistine. I approached Yvonne, prepared to plant a light kiss on her cheek and was amazed when she turned her head so that our lips met. John stood and smiled, and we shook hands vigorously. "Thanks for coming," I said. "Thanks for asking us," he replied.

After a long and exuberant supper, they piled back into their van, tossing over their shoulders promises of another reunion soon at their house. "How could we have been so wrong about each other?" I asked my wife afterward. Had some Irish curse been lifted? Had the passage of time contrived to make us forget our laments? Had we discovered our folly and sought each other's forgiveness? My wife's reply was more analytical. "We weren't wrong. But they were probably never as bad as we imagined. We've raised good and decent children, and so have they. We grew over the years, and so did they," she said. "Evelyn," I told her, "I'm almost ashamed by this, but I have to make an admission. I love your brother's family. I love every single one of them." "I believe it's mutual," she said. That day and the meetings that continued to follow remain one of the great mysteries and joys of my life.

Vacation

The first night of vacation I was awakened by plaintive moans from above. It must be one of the children, I thought, alarmed by the strange cast and slant of the room, windows where there had been none the night before, unexpected lights, foreboding shadows. The pitiful sounds continued as my newly stirred wife made her way up the spiral staircase and back down.

"Well, are they all right now?" I asked.

"The three of them are sleeping like logs," she said. "The groans you heard belong to a sea gull."

The next night before dawn, I heard the call of a rooster. "I know it's not my imagination and I don't think it's one of the children, but I think I'm hearing a rooster," I told my sleepy wife.

"I'm in charge of sea gulls; you handle the roosters," she said, returning to slumber.

That morning the children, ages four, six, and seven, and I greeted a friendly native, and I mentioned the sounds.

"Roosters? Sure are, and ducks and rabbits, too, right down the lane and take a left onto Fletcher."

There we found a barnyard. It became one of the many curious and gentle charms that made up the lure of a hamlet called Orient jutting into the sea at the end of Long Island, New York.

The night sounds continued and were joined by the chimes of the halyard's slap against mast and flagpole and the occasional furtive chug of a boat returning to port very late or slipping out very early.

I must admit the children discovered the pleasures of the hamlet long before the parents and then led us to them. Where we live most of the year, we see the neighbor on one side of our woods maybe once every two months, and I never met the neighbor on the other side. The children disappeared in Orient the very first day on an adventure of discovery—streets and alleys, a general store, an ice cream parlor, a vast field once occupied by Indians, a beach, a dock, people young and old who wanted to say hello and share their opinion of the quality of the day.

We at first were alarmed when they and the bikes were gone so long but soon got over it. Our cottage permitted a panoramic view of Orient Harbor. Being cosmopolitan and eyeing the second-story deck, we adults began gravitating upstairs in the early evening to sip cocktails as the sunset put on its show. The children showed us there was too much fun to be had at dusk, and we all began taking walks, exploring the handful of streets, greeting people, making small talk, wending our way home by the increasing number of routes we were learning. Before long, we had favorite walks, night and day, a special fishing spot, a house we particularly admired, a prospect we wouldn't tire of, new acquaintances, a cat who paid us visits.

The man who had rented us the cottage and then gone off to Europe was thoughtful and trusting. He gave us access to his house and garage. We became proprietary, making sure everything was just right, building an affection for his place and the community swifter and deeper than we realized. I met a man who was born in Beirut, as was my father. The next day I saw him coming as I walked home from the general store and hollered out, "Marhabah!" which is "hello" in Arabic. It was not the same man. "Hi," said this man, ignoring my strange greeting. It was the kind of gentle moment that occurred often.

Orient used to be called by other names. Early settlers, in what must have been a moment of atypical whimsy, renamed it to acknowledge they were about as far east as you get without stepping foot in another country. We fished and swam, played tennis, went clamming, were taken sailing, rowed, put on an outdoor dinner, went twice to other homes for cocktails. My wife ran in a road race.

We had intended to visit other communities, since we had vacationed elsewhere on the fork other summers, but we never seemed to find the time. When we went into Greenport, much larger and ostensibly more diverse, it was mostly for groceries, and we were eager to get back to Orient. We had trouble articulating the attraction, but it had to do with scale, with being able to enter into a tiny community, learn something about it and its people, and be "from Orient" for a little while.

It also had to do with age. Orient was proud of being old, revered its age, honored it ancestors, Indian and white. It had to do with an absence of affectation, unless pride in not being trendy or tony is itself an affectation. The attraction was elusive, and that in itself was part of the attraction.

In "downtown Orient," a handful of stores on Village Lane, the ice cream parlor was not open when the sun is high but only in the evening; one shop sold quilts and another herbs and spices. The Post Office architecture featured bloom-filled window boxes.

One day near the end of our vacation the children asked us to buy them a house of our own in Orient. The thought had already crossed our minds. Visiting a realtor seemed an obligatory part of any successful vacation, an attempt to possess a part of the place that gave so much pleasure. We learned the obvious: Houses on the market were few and far between; they were expensive when they did become available; house lots could be obtained, but finding one on one of our favorite little lanes was not too realistic.

We packed up, sorry to leave, and drove home, happy to be there, and before our first evening back was over, the children had presented themselves in the living room. "We've gotten all of our money from our banks and secret hiding places and want to give it to you for our house in Orient," said the eldest. "You don't have to count it. We did already, and it's $46.71."

I took the money, touched, and put it in an unused ceramic bank in the shape of a lion. I couldn't tell whether the children realized they had tapped a deep longing in their parents for such a house.

"Is that a lot of money, Dad?" asked another of the children.

"It's a great start, children," I told them, throwing myself headlong into the mission, "and if we keep feeding this lion we'll have our house in Orient before you know it."

They were thrilled, and they believed me. Craziest thing is, I was thrilled, and I still believe it myself.

Waiting

Curious how a memory, instead of fading, can grab you and never let go. I have such a memory of a neighborhood boy named Jason. I spent many years waiting for Jason. As I carried on my life, pursued a career, married successfully the second time, became a father, I was still waiting to hear he was finally okay.

Jason never knew of my vigil. I'm not sure why I was so compelled to carry it on. It didn't make any real difference. Jason died in humiliation, if he still had such feelings, in a bed in an insane asylum.

When I was six or eight years old and Jason was a budding teenager, we were part of a group of youngsters who would gather on a stoop or under a street lamp through the long evenings of summer and autumn, until the cold drove us apart and indoors until the next season.

Jason was tall and spare, wide at the shoulders, lean at the waist, with a broad, flat chest often partially exposed through his open-necked white shirt. His belt was too long, and the excess dangled down through a loop on his dark trousers. His black hair was straight and shiny, with a thick lock drooping, like his belt, and he had a black mole on the side of his chin.

I remember mostly Jason's smile, which could be shy or kind or sassy. He was neither particularly mean nor patronizing toward us younger children, but he would pay us his grownup's attention and smile to express his interest and pleasure. Jason made us feel pretty good.

One summer's eve under the street lamp or, more likely, in the undeveloped block of house lots that had become our secret forest, we got word that Jason was in the hospital. No one could figure out why. Of course, we began to try to find out from our parents, our older sisters and brothers and others in the neighborhood by listening with special care when Jason's name came up.

Jason had two brothers, one a contemporary of mine, so I spent time in their apartment, even after Jason's loud and angry father died. I always waited and listened for anything Jason's mother had to say about her eldest son, but she said nothing. There were no revelations—only her ironing, the frequent reaching into the breadbox, and the radio soap opera grinding on in the background.

All we could get—and all I ever got, even into my adulthood—was that Jason was clumsy around girls, that his parents signed him in and, as in some nightmarish tale, when they tried to get him out the state said, no, Jason's too dangerous, we must keep him locked up. What I feel must have happened to Jason was that he developed his mental illness—rage at his parents, debilitating confusion over his sexuality or whatever other sickness frightened the authorities into holding on to him—because he had been abandoned and caged at the moment in his life when he most ached to grow and be free.

Over the years, his mother told mine of visits with Jason, how Jason would curl up in a corner of the bed and refuse to move or utter a word until she left. "Poor woman, she doesn't need such grief," my mother would say. Many times over the next several decades, in many places, suddenly I would remember Jason, picture him frozen in his bed, his long legs bent like tent poles under the sheets, waiting blankly for his mother to shove the candy bars into his table drawer, ask how he was being treated, pack up her shopping bag and leave.

What a waste, what a waste, I would say, moist-eyed. One decision by his parents, one brief period of being embarrassed by Jason's coming of age, and they signed away his life.

Recently my family and I visited my parents, and I happened to pick up the ringing phone when no one else was nearby. It was Jason's elderly mother. I asked about her son Arthur, the engineer. He was just great, beautiful family, big business in Denver; she had flown out and back just last month.

And how about young Mal, my onetime chum. Probably not so successful as Arthur, because all she could say was "He's doing well, too," and then there was silence. I told myself, You never again will pick up a phone and be able to ask. Ask now.

"And what about Jason?" I was steady but on the verge of trembling.

"Poor Jason, he died, it's been twelve years ago," she said. That was all. I couldn't tell whether she was touched by the question or just felt she had to say something to close the subject. But she touched something in me. I couldn't be angry with her.

"Well, you did the best you could. It wasn't easy," I said.

I handed the phone over to my mother, left the room and began to sob such abundant tears I couldn't speak. My wife, alarmed by my condition, also began to cry, and she put her arm around my shoulder. In a few minutes I was fine. That's all Jason would ever have needed.

Street Corners

A well-dressed man, beyond middle age, is standing on a street corner in my old hometown as I come running up. I catch my breath, stretch my bare legs. It is cold. He is curious but cautious. I nod good morning.

"How far did you run?"

"Only three. Not in shape. Used to run twenty-six."

"I used to run. I was a boxer for four years. Fought out of Lynn."

Boxers, I happen to know, are warm and sentimental people. They only get mad in the ring. The really melancholy ones don't even get mad then. I have an affinity for them.

"You must've been good," I tell him, examining his face. "They never touched your nose."

He smiles at my assessment but intends to be perfectly honest. "You're right, but take a look at this scar." He points to a dark line over his left eye. "I got butted in a fight. It healed okay but it never went away."

My wife Evelyn runs up. We introduce ourselves and say we're visiting my parents with our three children. He knows my parents and where they live and tells me they're good people.

"I'm waiting for my wife to get ready. We'll go out for a ride, then a nice Chinese dinner." He names a restaurant I used to go to. "That's over by the Quincy police headquarters. For years after I left Boston I used to dream about the mountain of sweet and sour chicken they'd bring out."

He is getting interested in prolonging the talk but apparently doesn't care for sweet and sour chicken. He begins to talk about other food. Evelyn and I stretch and jog in place to stay warm.

"I am retired as a counterman at the G & G Delicatessen, you ever hear of it? Well, every politician had to come and eat at the G & G, and I met them all. I remember, one time Dwight D. Eisenhower shows up, he wants to be president. 'General,' I say to him, 'how do you take your corned beef, fat or lean?'

"The general says to me, 'You're the expert, I leave it to your discretion.' So I make him a beautiful sandwich on rye with a little mustard. Half fat, half lean. I watch him eat it, he really enjoys it. On his way out I say, 'General, how about a nice sandwich for the road?' and he says, 'Thank you, that was delicious and it was sufficient.'"

The man's wife appears. She is about his age and also carefully dressed. Heavy makeup suggests she is hiding something, maybe age, maybe sorrow. Her manner is decorous yet warm. Conversation reveals that she and I attended the same elementary school and even had some of the same teachers, though decades apart. I am excited by this connection to the past. "One day, I'll never forget it," she says, "I was passing Miss McNamara's room and looked in, and she was hugging Mr. Cameron, or he was hugging her, or they were hugging each other."

"She was single, and he was married!" I blurt out, deeply involved in her story.

"I know," she says, "And I've always wondered since exactly what that hug meant." We take turns guessing: a secret affair, her comforting him at the moment of some terrible news, his comforting her, celebrating a raise in pay. "And," continues the woman, further testing my memory, "do you remember Miss Cronin?"

"Crow-nose!" we shout simultaneously, the name given by generations of pupils to the skinny, severe teacher with the huge beak.

The husband has a schoolboy story he wants to tell. It is about the Battle of Lexington and Concord and his fear of being called on and giving the wrong answer.

"And sure enough she calls on me, and I have to stand up, and I'm so frightened, I'm shaking. 'Bernard,' she asks, 'what was the name of the foe in that battle?' I know the answer, of course, but I'm nervous, so for some reason I say as loud as I can, 'The British Boy Scouts!' And the whole class goes crazy." As he speaks, the man has turned red with ancient embarrassment, then overcomes it and is weaving back and forth with laughter, showing the gold teeth at the back of his mouth. "So the teacher says, 'Will you repeat for the class what you just said?' and maybe she meant I was to give the real answer but I say, 'The

British Boy Scouts' and the class goes crazy again and she says, 'Sit down, Bernard.'"

We enjoy the memory immensely, partly because it shows a youthful derision of the redcoats, and my wife and I seem to have forgotten we are cold.

"Marjorie," the man tells his wife, "they're visiting from New York. They have three little children inside with grandma and grandpa."

"Your sister was once our baby sitter," the wife says. "I heard she was a lovely young girl so I called up, and she came over and took care of our son."

"I'll tell her," I say. "She'll enjoy learning that we met."

"Did you ever hear of Dr. S___ in New York?" she asks. Her husband listens carefully but has no intention of joining in. I find the question naive but merely tell her I don't know him.

"He's a big doctor, they call him in on all the big cases. Our son had multiple sclerosis; he was eighteen years old already. We were referred to Dr. S____. He says, 'We have a new operation, let us do it, it'll give your son a better life.' He wanted it, too, but he was only eighteen, it was our decision.

"So we all go down to New York," she says, "and they take him in the operating room, and they operate on him, and they come out and tell us he is dead."

I look from face to face. My wife and I want to embrace them, hug each other, break into tears, do something, but the elderly couple is composed. They make it clear that they only want to warn us against using Dr. S____ in New York and that the subject is closed. They tell us they enjoyed the chat; we say the same.

A street corner in the old hometown. Life and death. Fat and lean.

Dinner with the Folks

"What can I do for you?" asked the waitress. Her tense face revealed, rather than a desire to serve, a need to complain that she was overworked and tired and, probably, suffering from a poor choice of shoes.

"Why am I blue?" answered my mother. Someone had approached her to offer help. My mother had responded by seeking an explanation for her vexing mood.

My father learned toward her, smiling but looking exasperated, to say the woman was only in charge of taking food orders.

"She'll have the schrod with a baked potato, no salad. The one on the luncheon special. It costs $5.95, with coffee and dessert," he said, pinning it down like a litigator. "I want the same, with salad, house dressing." I always waited to hear my father say schrod. I loved hearing it in the same way I loved the way he said "purdy" when he looked at my young daughter.

"Two scrod," said the waitress.

"What did she say?" asked my mother.

"She's getting the food," he said.

"Tell her to take care of the children first," said my mother. "Miss, take care of the children. They've driven two hundred miles to see us. Look at those little faces. It tears your heart out. They're starving."

I wondered twenty minutes later whether we were being punished by the weary waitress, being made to wait longer than necessary for our food, because my mother had a perfectly reasonable psychiatric question and my father had said schrod. Waiters in some of the best seafood houses in Boston said schrod. Tourists said scrod.

Did I dare tell the joke? Fellow jumps into a cab at Logan Airport. "Where to?" asks the driver. "Take me to a place to get scrod," says the visitor. "That's something," says the cabbie. "What's something?" says the visitor. "I never heard the past pluperfect before," says the driver.

We ate the mediocre food. I suspected my father chose this roadhouse because he associated it with a kinder time, a time not so long ago when he and my mother dressed up on Sunday, entered the restaurant, waved to friends, and dined graciously and without feeling financially reckless.

As we finished, I awaited with pleasure another ritual. My father excused himself, only to return five minutes later, smiling but red-faced. "It was my turn to pay," he protested. "When," he asked, "were you able to see the bill?" Sometimes he became so genuinely upset that I let him pay but ended up feeling vaguely exploitive. Children, I feel, are not supposed to manipulate their parents for a restaurant dinner.

On the way back to the home, my mother wanted to know how they made the fish so tough. My father excused her rudeness, saying the fish was fine. She was surrounded by her family and despite the indigestible dinner was happy and broke into "Auld Lang Syne." Her sentimental joy was infectious. We all sang.

But a few minutes later she thought of an airplane that blew up in the sky over Scotland. "It makes me cry," she said, and, for a few moments, she mourned for the victims. After a while, she felt like talking again. "I don't want to die," she declared. A decade ago everyone in the car would have raced to tell her to stop talking so foolishly. But this, we knew, was a different language, requiring a different sensitivity.

"Why don't you want to die, Mother?" asked my wife.

My mother's voice was strong. "Because I want to stick around and cause some trouble," she said. She had caught us. We all laughed.

"God bless you, Ma," I said. "Long may you deliver your priceless sucker punches."

I thought back to the first time my wife-to-be and my parents met. "I thought you were a solid man, a good person," she said afterward, "but it wasn't until I met your parents that I really wanted to marry you."

In the nursing home room, my father sat with his wife on the edge of the bed. He gently pulled her skirt down over her knees. He held her hand in both of his, leaned toward her and kissed her forehead. He blushed. "She won't remember a thing about this tomorrow," my father said. His statement was both assurance that she did not hurt so deeply and a complaint that all our love was ultimately in vain.

"*We'll* remember," I told him.

Many Happy Returns

On the morning of my recent birthday the rain stopped and the sun broke through. My wife and three young children surrounded me in the living room and proffered gifts: a forest-green cotton sweater, a twin pack of Reese's Peanut Butter Cups, allowance money returned to cover movie tickets, an after-shave product that calmed the skin. It was wonderful, but another thought persisted. "I've got to call my parents," I said and dialed them long-distance.

"Happy Birthday," said my father, who is more than eighty, when he heard my voice.

"Dad, I'm calling because it occurs to me that this day may be more important to you than to me."

"I don't remember details," he began, but he did. "When you were born, we had the store on Broadway next to the theater in Washington Heights. A friend rushed in and told me I had a boy, my first boy. I was excited. I called you my Latin from Manhattan." He sounded happy and thanked me for calling.

I telephoned my mother, who lives in a nursing home a few miles from my father's house.

"Darling, many happy returns," she said, as she has for a half-century. I told her I considered this her day as well as my own. "Well, you were supposed to be born early in the afternoon," she began, "but the doctor came to my room and said 'Please don't have your baby for a few more hours. The Yankees are in the World Series and I've got tickets to today's game.'"

I'd heard the story before but love hearing it.

"So he went to the ballgame and came back and asked how I felt. And I said, 'Oh, doctor, I can't wait much longer.' So he said, 'Get ready, we're taking you to the delivery room to have your baby.'"

Her old woman's memory, which sometimes fails her, leaving her crying in frustration, seemed infallible for venerable events, and she spoke with comfortable authority.

"Here's the funny part. I was in a semi-private room, and the woman in the other bed, she was young and pretty but a little dumb, was listening to every word. And when she heard the doctor say I was going to have my baby, she jumped up. 'Hey,' she said, 'that's not fair. I was here first.'"

My mother laughed; the sound of ancient, undeniable pleasure came through the receiver.

On some birthdays I had succumbed to a dismal exercise—listing my shortcomings, indulging in a no-win game of personal stocktaking.

No such foolishness this time. I had stumbled onto something profound. I had traveled back to my literal birth day. And, boy, did I have fun!

Piety

I cried again a few days ago for the ugly boy. I had thought that my sorrow over him and our meeting was all used up, but now I realize it's as strong as ever.

It was three years ago that my father walked me to a spacious tent near his home. The tent was his idea when the Jews of his suburban outpost found themselves facing the High Holy Days without a proper house of worship. I was impressed and proud of him as he showed me around: the ark with its eternal light where the Torah scrolls were kept, the table from which the rabbi and cantor would lead the service, the row upon row of folding seats, and the velvet ropes and floral bouquets that gave the temple an elegance, even a sense of permanence.

As we withdrew to inspect the outside of the tent, my father disclosed that there had been trouble from some local boys. They had cut their way in, upset some of the equipment, may have stolen small items. The police had come, noted the problem and left, he said, but the trouble had continued. I felt my pride hardening into anger. Suddenly, on the least visible side of the tent, at the edge of hilly woods, we spotted two figures trying to enter. I ran toward them shouting, offended by their desecration, forecasting their discomfort in the next world, threatening to reduce them to a pulp.

Two teenagers looked up, startled but unafraid. When I spied a bare branch on the ground—my staff!—and began wielding it, they became concerned but seemed still reluctant to flee. I noticed in my rising fury that one of the boys was incredibly handsome and that his friend was woefully ill-made—eyes sunken, nose pressed to one side, forehead bulging.

"Stay where you are, don't run!" I challenged them. "The cops will find both of you, dead or unconscious." I raised the branch with two hands over my head, as if to crack it down over theirs. "All I have to do is say you were trying to damage the temple and steal what was inside!" They leaped up, finally frightened, not at the enormity of their crimes or my accusations, I felt, but at the prodigious energy I bore against them. The boys began to walk off resentfully, each looking worried that the other would consider him a coward. They did not move fast enough for me.

"Get going, damn you! Yes, you, you moron!" I shouted at the handsome one. "And you," I said, turning to the other one, "never let anyone see your hideous face here as long as you live!"

Even as those last words were in flight, I was sorry. Any notion that I'd done a good deed was swept away. My father said nothing then or later, trying, I suspect, to spare me further pain. Why did I have to humiliate the boy? Why did I want to add to his misery? I realized that I'd gone crazy—crazy with zeal.

Then the boys were gone; there was nothing else I could say to them. The boys and the tent and the words and my father's silence filled my head. It was one of the many times I would cry for the boy.

But this time, on the High Holy Days a few days ago, I cried for myself as well. I asked for forgiveness and prayed that the boy understood. It was not his ugliness that was revealed at the temple, it was mine.

Salim the Shopkeeper

The *New York Times* reported that a car loaded with more than one-hundred pounds of explosives blew up in the Christian area of Beirut, in front of a bakery where people had lined up to buy bread. The blast came as life in the city was returning to normal after three days of artillery and rocket exchanges between Muslim and Christian forces.

I read the account with the dull feelings of pity and confusion and helplessness I always feel about the warfare in Lebanon. I searched for the names of victims or survivors to give the violence some context.

Perhaps Maryam was buying extra loaves for a birthday party for her young son. Farid wanted to please his ailing wife, who loves the smell of fresh bread. Widad was planning a special lunch for her visiting parents. Samir was buying extra supplies for friends in his office. This way I could look again at the story and understand the terror and tragedy.

A few hours later Charles, who is ten years old, and I approached a Middle Eastern grocery store in a large city in the northeast section of the United States to buy, among other things, fresh loaves of the round bread. Charles' grandfather had just celebrated his eighty-fourth birthday. We would bring bread, stuffed vine leaves, the eggplant salad called baba ghanouj, the mashed chick peas and sesame paste known as hummus bi tahina, and purple olives as large as young plums.

It was food we all loved because it tasted good and because it was a form of communication. It brought together the old man, his son, and the son of his son. The food was one thing that continued to make sense to a man born in Beirut, an Arab in almost every way, yet a tenacious Jew, an altogether curious breed in a yet more curious world.

The store never failed to excite me a little. "Look, Charles," I said, "we're in the souk, the bazaar, welcome to the casbah." Salim the shopkeeper was nowhere to be seen. I tried to imagine the store as my son saw it. Did he notice first the serving platters and utensils and water pipes, brassware and copper, glassware and hammered silver, on the high shelves at the back of the store? Or the neat, geometric middle shelves, given over to row of cans and jars and boxes of groceries? Fresh vegetables were at the left wall; tubs of halvah, trays of fresh spinach and meat pies, coffee beans, nuts, pastries, bins of lentils on the right. At the front, near the counter and cash register, were Arabic magazines, books, and tapes.

I looked into Charles's guileless, sunny face and into his large brown eyes and saw for a moment my beloved Uncle Charlie, in the old country I'd never known, seated cross-legged in a lavish dining room, surrounded by his family, happy and secure. Since it was a mirage, it was gone in an instant, like a photograph tucked back into a drawer.

Charles looked back at me and said, "Dad, am I permitted to buy a pack of gum?" I love him for many reasons, not the least being his honesty and his good manners. He fetched a plastic hand basket, and we began to shop.

Salim appeared from the rear of the store, patting his mouth as he discreetly transferred an olive pit to a cupped hand. I told him about my father, about his birthday, and that he'd taken a tumble on a slippery sidewalk. "When they are old," he said, without detectable emotion, "it is bad, very bad." He refrained from saying what he meant, that an old person' fall can be a prelude to death.

Salim was a curious man. He was capable of kindness, but over time he had become aloof. When we first brought our children to Salim's store seven years ago, he reached into a jar and came up with a fistful of treats. "This is America," he said. "We are free. The candy should be free." We all enjoyed him. I had encouraged the children to call him "Uncle Salim." But more recently, he appeared angry and bitter, unbecoming traits in anyone, particular a shopkeeper.

I had begun to reflect on the change. I wondered about the irregular scar that ran across his right cheek from the side of the nose to the edge of the mouth. Maybe he fell off a bike as a boy in Lebanon, I speculated, but that wasn't very satisfying. I weighed whether he had been hurt in the country's long strife, but in a war of bullets and bombs had trouble imagining how. I felt I couldn't ask him so decided on the following: As a young man, tall and handsome as he is now, he sat one afternoon at a sidewalk café sipping Turkish coffee with friends when a beautiful young woman and her mother walked by. Salim's eyes strayed to the daughter. He looked her up and down, and his gaze was noticed. That night the girl's brothers found Salim. "I can't marry your sister," he pleaded. "I already have a wife." They held him down and hurt his face. "Next time," they said, "we will cut lower."

It was clear to me from looking into Salim's brooding eyes that he was not by choice a shopkeeper on the outskirts of a new city in a strange country. His manner revealed pride and vanity. I sensed that if we ever sat down with a bottle of arak, the powerful anise-flavored liquor, between us, I would learn that Salim had aspired to be a political leader, perhaps the man who would heal his country. But since it was unlikely we would ever meet outside his store, and increasingly obvious he was concealing everything about himself but his moodiness, I clung to my imagined story of romance and violence, like Lebanon itself.

In the past, when we visited the store with my father, he and Salim spoke in fervent, melodic Arabic. But asked later about Salim and his past, my father said he knew nothing about him, not even his religion, only that he spoke with a Lebanese accent and said he was from Beirut. The last time my father and I shopped together, Salim looked our way and turned away without a sign of recognition. By the time we brought our purchases to the counter, he had slipped out of the store, leaving us to make strained inquiries to his soft-spoken, blonde-haired wife. Outside, my father said he was upset at the snub and suggested that next time we try Salim's competitor.

The new store itself rankled Salim. His own first store, on a busy thoroughfare near an intersection, allowed for very little parking. So it was with high expectation that he relocated in a small shopping center with its own parking lot. Many people, we included, turned out to admire the new shop and wish him good luck and buy extra foods and supplies. But not long after that, another Middle East grocery opened near Salim's original location.

Salim's merchant instinct should have lead him to say, "We all love the Arabic food; there is plenty of business for both of us," or to playfully challenge his customers, "Go and visit the new man, I'm not worried. I think I'll see you tomorrow." But he began instead to accuse his competitor of treachery, of lowering the price on one item and inflating it on another, less for a jar of vine leaves, more for rice and spices and nuts. And when recently my father bargained with Salim over the price of his goods, a traditional and respected way of life for Middle Eastern people, Salim became impatient and inflexible.

Strangest of all was the Spam. Salim introduced the cans of ground pork parts to his store. I have never heard of a call for Spam. I had never seen anyone reach for it. He arranged several Spam cans on the shelf, not discreetly in the back but near the front of the store. Knowing pork is an anathema to many people, nonetheless in one insane stroke he puzzled his small Jewish clientele and declared war on his substantial number of Muslim customers.

The last time I dropped in by myself, he became atypically animated and talkative. But it was more a strained monologue than a conversation. No longer preoccupied with the Muslims, he railed against what he called "the Jew people," the problems they had caused to his homeland, how only the United States, where so recently the candy was free, could control the Jews and solve the problems. Salim knew I was a Jew. I was angered by what he said, but at the same time moved by his apparent self-immolation in the troubles of Lebanon, his hopeless longing for a homeland forever changed. My father said he himself had dismissed all serious concern for Lebanon a generation ago; last year, he told me he dreamed he was back in Beirut.

This day, Charles and I quietly finished our shopping. Salim, as was his custom, set up a shopping bag below the cash register and rang up each item before carefully lowering it into the bag. He was silent and unsmiling. We paid and began to leave. Charles turned and looked up at Salim and said, "Good-bye, Uncle Salim."

The shopkeeper seemed stunned. "Good-bye," he said to both of us after a long pause. Then he ran around the counter and came close to Charles, looking down at him and reaching out with a sesame candy. "Good-bye, Honey" he said.

The people in the bakery were dead. I didn't know if Lebanon itself would survive. But in that moment, I knew that Salim would.

Burdens

The party was over, the ship under way. Gaiety would flow for seven days, but every reveler carried the baggage of tragedy still. This was a voyage of widows and other women alone, except for the gallery of relatives, contemporary and adolescent, that had tagged along for the sail.

The immense Dutch ship, with its crew of ingratiating Indonesians, did not intend the cruise between New York and Bermuda to be for widows. But their predominance was as evident as the colors the ship flew. There were the freshly arranged silver thatches and kindly heads, an eagerness to break into song, the courtly abundance of praise and flattery, to each other and their bon-voyage visitors. There was the wealth of food and drink foisted on the well-wishers, an almost frenzied effort to make certain no belly was less than full, no gullet dry.

There also was the swift look between widows that one wasn't supposed to see, the veiled lament lurking behind the eyes, the name of the loved one or the despised one whose name was never uttered. There was the uproarious laughter coaxed by the most cautious joke. There was, never to be seen, the tears meant for no outsiders.

My wife and I and our three children had a special role to play. It was to pay tribute to my mother-in-law and demonstrate, by our presence and generosity, how important and special she was. The other mothers had arranged for the precise same treatment, so the only difference became how many attendants each widow had and what the attendants bestowed in food and drink. Yet the lavishness of the party and the excited crush of people aboard stood as an ironic testament to the hollowness that the guests of honor felt on so many other days and nights.

I knew from a previous dockside party the nature of the business at hand and admitted feelings of discomfort to my wife. I didn't care to be part of the sham, although I realized the importance of the event to my wife's mother. So I went, not to pay tribute to my mother-in-law so much as to honor the wishes of my wife. I wished everyone well. I drank as well or better than the rest of the party. When my mother-in-law mentioned she had bought a jump rope to lose weight before the trip, I stepped into the conversation. "You're supposed to take it and tie it around the refrigerator," I said blithely. She was proud of my wit. She repeated it to the other ladies. The other ladies laughed.

Someone said something critical about the champagne we had brought, which in fact was far superior to their Finger Lakes soda pop. I was there to pay tribute, not argue. I kept quiet. Several visitors to the party left without a farewell. Perhaps they felt they had an obligation to carry out, and it didn't include courtesy to me. I kept the insult to myself. We left the ship, with three tired and excited children, and my wife began to tell me of the emotional baggage that is a stowaway wherever these women go.

"Patricia's husband was a bigamist. He just disappeared one day. She tried to have him traced, but I don't know what happened. He's dead now. Or as good as." Patricia's entourage had included her daughter, son-in-law, and a man named Jim.

"Jim, he's the quiet one, was brought up by Patricia. His real mother died of cancer as a young woman. His father couldn't take the loss. He got so depressed, they put him in the hospital. They made the mistake of putting him on the sixth floor because one day he jumped out the window."

There had been a woman seated in a chair during the entire party. "That was Margaret. She has a husband, but he couldn't come. His foot was just removed. His condition could get worse."

"Elizabeth lost her husband a long time ago, to a German bullet in World War I. She was still a girl but already with a large family. Elizabeth was supposed to marry again. But a few days before the wedding, her fiancé fled the town."

And on it went. My mother-in-law lost her railroad man husband not to some great mechanical catastrophe but to gnawing illness. He died in the driveway of his home one bitter cold night as his family struggled to get him an ambulance. I never met him. My wife will always miss him. She wanted our first son to be named Edward after him. I chose the middle name and tucked away my list for another time.

Now the ship was gone. The women would be resting and chatting and primping for this first dinner out. I leave them with my own special wish, as intense and unspoken as the lament behind the kindly eyes. When you are far away, and there is no land in sight and it is for the moment only you and vastness around you, may you lift your burdens and cast them into the sea.

Bullies

I came to fatherhood thoroughly experienced with bullies but poorly trained to teach my children how to deal with them. For my mother, by comparison, bullies were a favorite subject. She despised them yet loved taking them on. They gave her the chance to show her mettle and fill me with her impressive but impractical advice. "Once they start up with you," she would say, "beat them at their own game. Grab a board. Hit them in the shins. Get a rock. Bring it down over their heads." Delivering this wisdom, she became animated and red-faced. To my knowledge she never picked up a rock, but I did witness her reducing bullies to a constitutional pulp.

In our blue-collar neighborhood, she rang aggressors' doorbells, not knowing whether kindness or cruelty lay behind the door. Sometimes she confronted the bullies on the street, usually to redress an affront or an assault against me. "What is it about us that you don't like?" she might ask. "Is it the color of my little boy's hair (touching my head as I huddled, fascinated, by her skirt)? Is it our religion?"

By this time the bully or, often as not, his equally belligerent father, was reduced to a series of nods. "Well, then," she would conclude, "be our friends or leave us alone in peace." Years later, when I asked if she had stolen her speech from Shakespeare, my mother became annoyed and said to stop acting like the big shot who reads too many books. But I have not, in a lifetime of trying, built such a comparable armor against the bully. I once thought I had. I once thought there wasn't a bully in the world who could bluff me into fear or miserable subjugation.

A long time ago, at night on the street, I was surprised by a group of boys led by an older girl. They surrounded me, and the girl tried to taunt me into insulting or slapping her, which I understood, would be the cue for her horde to pounce. I watched for an opportunity and punched one of the boys, opening the circle for my escape. In a schoolyard, I actually chased a bully once and he ran away, and even as I raced after him I wondered what to do if I caught him. But I did catch up and the bully spun to face me. "Say, you're fast," he said, smiling. "You ought to join our track team."

A generation later I ran into a former boyhood bully in a tavern in Greenwich Village, New York. There is, even among uncongenial old acquaintances, a kind of affection and nostalgia, and that is what I felt for him. But after a few minutes I was sorry to learn he hadn't changed. He smirked and asked about the boys I used to hang around with, the ones he and his gang could terrify at will by merely walking up close and staring. I said, "You can buy me a beer or join me outside for the whipping of your life." I was so glad I said whipping. I don't use the word as a rule but it was a favorite of my mother's during instructions in bully warfare. One might think that was the moment to look the bully straight in the eye, but I gazed instead into the mirror behind the bar to make certain that I was doing the talking. The bully, looking forlorn, flagged down the bartender. It was, to be sure, the most savory beer of my life.

My batting average against bullies has been .400; in an exceptional season, maybe .500. I'd never shaken off the fear, not of the bullies themselves but of confrontation. The rewarding tavern incident should have taught me better, but I later lost a bout in a corporate showdown. I failed because I knew that what I wanted to say would upset my antagonists: "Ladies and gentlemen, your position is unprofessional and insensitive and, while the subject's on the floor, generally ludicrous." I despised my own quiet compliance.

On the subways, I became the first to blink in any eyeballing contest. My wife made me promise. "Don't win the contest and get killed for it," she said, "What would happen to us?" So I came to fatherhood incompletely equipped to teach my two young sons and daughter how to cope with bullies. Naturally a bully appeared at our doorstep, quickly sensed the vulnerability in the household, and started to take over.

Carl was only about thirteen years old, a year older than Edward and two more than Charles, but he was as big as their father and, judging from his physique, twice as strong. He wore his T-shirts with the sleeves rolled up to expose his perpetually tanned shoulders. He favored wet-looking crew cuts and carried the trademark smirk of invincibility. If

I were casting a movie, I'd have hired him to play the sadistic drill sergeant in charge of an army barracks in a steamy backwater of the Deep South.

During our brief conversation, he talked with ease about the bores of rifles, steel-tipped arrows, survival in the woods, the best ammunition for bringing down small game, the pleasures of dressing a freshly killed ten-point deer. Edward was impressed. When I asked Carl where all this action took place, he became vague. "Upstate. My dad and I go. It's great. Sometimes we don't even bother to sleep in the cabin. We camp in the woods. I want to get me a big brown bear."

"Liar! Fake!" I wanted to shout at him. He seemed to know I wouldn't. He chewed his gum and smiled.

He began telephoning, never identifying himself. I'd instructed the boys and their nine-year-old sister Sara never to brook incivility or impoliteness on the phone. "If a person is not willing to identify himself or is otherwise rude, simply hang up. I don't care if it's a child or an adult asking for me." My wife heartily agreed.

Charles answered the telephone one evening. "Who is this, please?" he asked. "Put Edward on," the voice said. He hung up. Carl called back immediately. To my consternation, Edward was concerned that Carl might be upset. I didn't hear the conversation but his tone was placating.

There began a series of weekend nights when it became imperative for Edward to go to the movies in a neighboring community. I sensed that Carl was demanding Edward's company there. Edward, of compact frame, handsome and with a quiet, flirtatious manner, was probably the lure that Carl needed to get the attention of the girls they knew from school.

One night after the movies I drove Edward and three of the girls home. Carl lived in the other direction and had been picked up. "Oh, gross," one of the girls said in the back seat. The others agreed, "Yeah." They were discussing Carl.

"I noticed," I told them, "that the marquee said your film was rated PG-13. Did everyone here have parental approval?" They thought that was funny and laughed. But Edward was silent. He was suffering. First his mentor Carl came under attack; then his father talked like a fool. My first-born son was only twelve and, at that moment, I felt the emptiness of his slipping away.

Carl's right to bully was not only encouraged, it was applauded. He played on a Little League team that competed with the team that included both Edward and Charles. Sara was on a club for younger children. At bat, Carl looked like a giant in a fairy tale, prepared to club any ball that came near him. On the mound he was even more intimidating. Some batters simply lost their nerve at his often inaccurate but always blistering fast balls. They swung three perfunctory times, dropped their heads, and walked to the dugout in shame. Others tried—each one a spunky little David facing Goliath—but they rarely connected.

My wife Evelyn and I watched a game early one evening, as insects at a nearby stream grouped, attacked, retreated, and swarmed again. The fans were eager to go home. Carl and his team were winning 15–0, and there was talk of a forfeit. When Edward came to bat, I thought, he and Carl are buddies, Carl will lighten up, he needs Edward to talk to the girls at the movies. But I was wrong. Carl wound up and hurled his pitches so fast I feared for my son's safety. Edward waited out a few pitches but he seemed as paralyzed as the rest. His patience, however, earned him a walk, and he trotted to first base. This annoyed Carl, who became even more intent on striking out the rest of the lineup.

A few batters later, with two outs, Charles stepped to the plate. Smaller than Edward and less confident in manner, he had been placed at the bottom of the order, where he could do the least harm. He set his feet and looked out at Carl and awaited his fate. Evelyn seized my hand anxiously. "Strike one!" shouted the large, good-natured umpire behind the plate. Parents in the stands looked at each other discreetly, avoiding our eyes, nodding that the inevitable was about to happen.

"Strike twooo!" I was not fearful for Charles as I had been for his brother. There was something in his stance—anger, defiance, courage, foolishness?—that was reassuring.

The next ball smoked in as fast as the others, Charles pulled in his chin, lifted and replanted his right foot and swung. Carl leaped straight up into the air. The ball, the glorious ball, shot just over his head, beyond the second baseman, and sailed back to earth on the outfield grass. Charles scurried to first base and on to second as his brother crossed the plate.

Parents screamed, "Charlie! Charlie!" and stomped their feet on the metal bleacher seats. They reached over to shake our hands. "Where did he learn to hit like that?" someone asked. "What a player!" "He's a secret weapon." The final score was 15–1.

Carl's clutch on Edward soon vanished. Charles took his new notoriety in stride. The lesson in dealing with bullies had come at an unlikely time from an unlikely source, but it was a lesson no one in our family would soon forget. I could hardly wait to tell my mother the news.

Baseball

The woman in front of us raised a flattering hand. In the great sweep of the stadium—darting colors, echoing sounds, bellowed emotions—the gesture was inconspicuous, resembling nothing more than a confused and wounded bird. Across the aisle, a handsome young dark man with a thin mustache and a small gold earring whistled and yelled "Soda!" An overweight middle-aged vendor with a large metal case containing only one cup of cola lumbered up the concrete steps. He handed it to Mr. Fairbanks who said, "Where's my straw?"

"For two dollars, you don't get one," said the vendor. The man began to drink. "Soda Man," I shouted, "come back with more." He nodded without conviction and left. "Dad," my young son Charles said suddenly, after what seemed to be a long rumination, "I have to get a ball."

It was the last day of the baseball season. New York was playing Detroit, and neither would qualify for the playoffs and postseason glory or riches. The weather was mercifully warm and windless, the fans prepared to overlook small indiscretions but eager for something or someone to blame for the Yankees' dismal performance.

The left fielder bobbled for a second consecutive time a ball slapped toward him, allowing the Tigers to take the lead. Vast grumblings of disgust rose and enshrouded him, as if condemning him to the minors. A third ball, hard-struck, sailed toward him. There was a common silence among twenty thousand people, a mass holding of breaths. The fielder held up his glove, and the ball thwacked safely into its pocket. The stadium erupted into exaggerated and derisive cheers.

The soda man reappeared with a full case of cola cups. The woman in front of us purchased one. I bought one for Charles, although he protested, in a grownup fashion, that he had his own funds and would like to treat me. Someone several aisles away to our right bought four. I was relieved that the soda man hadn't been summoned in vain.

"Watch Mattingly," said the man behind us. "He always takes the first pitch, and it's always a strike."

"But if that's so," I said, turning and welcoming the discussion, "every pitcher in the major leagues must know it." The man seemed to find my comment obvious but smiled. He wore a dark blue T-shirt with the gold insignia of the Fire Department of New York.

Don Mattingly, number 23, the great first-baseman and, for the eleven-year-old Charles, the most beloved figure in organized baseball, watched a fast ball zip by. The umpire shook his right fist at some imaginary threat, calling the strike.

A hot dog man, also middle-aged, arrived. I was amused by his subtle but stylized routine. From years in the stadium, his moves had come to simulate those of a pitcher. Delivering a customer's change, he first brought his arm straight back and then shot his hand out crisply, in the manner of a fastball. Handing over a frankfurter in a bun and a paper sleeve, he slid out his arm, elbow close to the ribs, a tricky maneuver with a speed not easy to read. When I was a boy, the hot dog man also pasted his hot dogs with a mustard brush, imitating the umpire dusting off home plate. The man with the thin mustache bought two franks for himself, demanding extra mustard packs, which he got, and napkins, which were wherever the straws were. Charles pointed out that there was no coordination between the arrival of the soda man and the hot dog man.

"I think most of the young sellers have returned to school by now. These guys do the best they can," I told him. I sounded like one of those public service messages for not dropping out of school.

I was on especially good behavior, working hard to regain the state of grace that is occasionally joyously accomplished between my son and me. I had promised him—promised, a sacred act—a Yankees baseball game all spring and summer. Then, a few days earlier, I had learned from the newspapers that the season would end with the Sunday afternoon game. Charles witnessed my dilemma. He waited until I was alone one evening and entered the bedroom. "Dad, if it's too much trouble, we'll get to go next season," he said. Naturally that moment of selflessness doomed me. I juggled work schedules, tried to think of people I knew with sports connections. The next morning I called Yankee Stadium. A hint of misery came through the telephone when the clerk told me tickets were available for all sections for the last game.

On Friday, I dropped my work, drove to the stadium, and bought the best tickets still available. They were box seats, not behind first base, near to Mr. Mattingly, but in right field, not far from a player named Mel Hall. I broke the news of the tickets to Charles. He told me later, on the ride to the stadium, he hadn't slept well for two nights looking forward to the pleasures of Sunday. And now, at the game, with the Yankees trailing, he declared a single, impossible hope: A batter would swing mightily, the ball would sail up in a great arc and descend into the stands, where it would find the pocket of his Little League glove as the fans around him danced and lunged in admiration and envy. This is how he would get his ball.

I weighed this possibility and tried to save him from too great a disappointment: "Charles, you have to realize the chances of the ball coming your way are one in thousands."

"Not that much," was his reply. He watched every pitch and swing and trajectory of the ball as if reading the cover to see if his name were stamped on it.

Something happened to bolster his dream. Mel Hall, after jogging out to right field at the top of each inning and tossing with other players, started to flip the balls to the crowd. Charles decided that if a batted ball was not delivered to his glove, one of Mel Hall's would.

He raced down to the railing, Yankee cap askew, gloved hand at the ready, to implore Mr. Hall with his eyes. Could I help? I wondered. Could I go with him, shout to the ballplayer, plead with him to recognize my son?

A ritual evolved. Inning after inning, as soon as the Yankees headed out of the dugout and onto the field, Charles ran down the steps to wait. And as his wish became more hopeless, his dream became bolder. Stuck in his shirt pocket was a pen, tested for writing on leather. Charles would persuade Mr. Hall, suddenly a hero outshining even the great Mr. Mattingly, to approach the railing and autograph both his glove and his newly acquired baseball.

The day of the last game of the decade grew old. The sun disappeared in a chalky sky, a breeze took a helium balloon up and over the wall.

The man with the mustache deserted the stands, leaving a heap of trash. The young woman at our left, whose large bosom pushing against her Yankees blouse had been a pleasant distraction for several innings, buttoned her pride inside a cardigan. The fireman, philosophic, said next year had to be better. He reached down and gave Charles his souvenir Yankees mug.

The imposing size of the stadium, the small dramas swirling in every corner, the thousands of people, the sorry performances of the former champions, the screeching of "The Star-Spangled Banner" (the right palm feeling the heart beat, the heart beating faster), combined with the bogus gayety of "Take Me Out to the Ballgame," the 3–5 losing score and the quest of my son, left me in a strange and emotional state. Charles's feelings, however, were uncomplicated and uncompromising.

"Dad, I have to get a ball and take it home," he said.

"Dear, it doesn't look like it's going to happen," I had to tell him. It was the top of the ninth, and Mr. Hall returned to right field. Charles was in position at the railing. Mr. Hall completed his warm-up, turned, and flipped the ball. It flew toward Charles and, from my seat forty feet away, I admired the way he stood his ground among a score of hopefuls, awaiting his destiny. A tall man directly behind him wearing a plaid flannel shirt and a down vest stood suddenly and took in the ball with two cupped hands.

Charles returned to his seat. I looked at him carefully. He still had summer freckles on his cheeks. His dark brown eyes, far from sad, blazed with excitement. "I said to Mel Hall, 'Mel, would you please come up and sign my glove?' and he stopped and looked up at me and said, 'What, what is it?' But then the umpire shouted 'Play Ball!' and he had to go."

On the way out of Yankee Stadium, we stopped at the gift shop and I bought him a baseball. He said thank you and that it cost a lot. We returned home, and I thought what a great day it had turned out to be. Charles may lose the baseball in a week or a month or on the first warm day of next spring. But we won't forget Mr. Hall of the New York Yankees, on the last day of a losing season, his kind face squinting, looking up and asking what he could do for my son.

The Thinking Place

"Daddy, come with me," said my daughter. She led me out of the house, down the slope of our backyard and into the woods. I was seldom a visitor here. I liked not knowing too much about the woods. I liked them to remain mysterious, full of wonderful, even fearful, events and creatures.

"Where are we going, Sara?" I asked, amused by her deliberate stride.

"You'll see," she said.

When the house was barely visible through the maples, oaks, hickories, black birches, and the thick wild grape vines that climbed them to the sunlight, Sara reached a spot she appeared to recognize, turned left and beckoned me to follow. As I caught up, she took my hand. In a few moments we arrived at a clearing. It measured ten feet square or so and had been swept clean. On opposing borders had been set two large smooth rocks. She sat down on one and nodded toward the other. I sat down across from her. On her face was the smug look of a child who knows she has succeeded in intriguing an adult.

Friends say I dote on my nine-year-old daughter and eventually will spoil her beyond redemption. I don't agree. I waited for her through one marriage and well into another. The first marriage was childless. To the second came two boys, both fair and handsome, then Sara. Even as an infant I saw in her dark eyes and features a Levantine temperament, intelligent and excitable. I began to call her "my little Arab" as a fanciful tribute to the region where my father and forefathers were born. I admit I am fascinated by her, but I am also fascinated by her brothers for many other reasons as well.

"Do Edward and Charles know about this?" I asked.

"No," she said. "No one does except me, and now you." The intimacy of the admission embarrassed her. She looked away.

"Well, all I can say is, it's beautiful here and peaceful, and you've done a remarkable job making the ground smooth …"

"Daddy," she interrupted, looking me again in the eyes, "this is my thinking place." She made it sound like an institution, a place spelled with capital letters. It was immediately clear that to her this makeshift cloister had about it something sacred.

"Sara, darling, I'm honored," I said, and it was the truth. "Tell me, how often do you come down to The Thinking Place?"

"It depends," she said. She shifted on her rock to tuck her knees under her chin and tugged at her overall strap to make it less snug. "If I have something on my mind I come here, or if the boys are being fresh or, you know, difficult, I come here."

How bright, I said to myself, for a child so young to understand the need for a place to get away to, and then to create such a place on her own. I wondered where she would go when winter came and her place was cold and covered with dead leaves. She watched me look around. "I think I know what you're thinking," she said with a grin. "I have a thinking place for bad weather, too. It's built of boxes in the attic. It's in the room behind where you type all the time." And so she surprised me for a second time.

"As long as we're relaxing here," I began, "with no one to bother us, not even your intelligent and good-looking, though treacherous and insensitive, brothers, do you have anything special on your mind?"

She chided me for the playful tone of the question. "Be serious. I want to ask you something," she said. I nodded and waited.

"Daddy, if you hadn't been married before, would I look different?"

The question amazed and confused me. I had to smile at its ingenuity, at the balance of thoughts and feelings, the connections that must have gone into its formation. I looked for a question within the question. Did she feel her looks were inadequate? Was this a criticism of her mother's looks or of mine? Was the question a complaint, a compliment? She had never asked about my first wife. To my knowledge, she was only vaguely aware that I had been married to anyone but her mother.

Whatever the question stood for, it made me realize what I had long suspected—that children lead two lives, the one they present routinely to their family and teachers and the secret one they reserve for themselves and perhaps their closest friends. For the moment, I felt I had become one of those closest friends.

"I'm glad you asked me, I'm pleased that you feel comfortable enough to talk to me about it," I said, and launched into an answer.

"I would be with my first wife to this day," I began, feeling an obligation to take a moral stand on marriage, "if we hadn't ending up fighting so much. It became a terrible and sad marriage. I remember coming home one night, putting the key in the door, and walking in. I felt a burden, as if an invisible giant was pushing down on my shoulders. I remember saying, 'There is a total absence of joy in this house.' Do you understand, Sara? Having fun had become impossible. Then I told her to tell everyone that she was leaving me. I thought at the time that was the honorable thing to do."

I stopped to gauge her interest, and she coaxed me to continue.

"Her name was Cynthia [a name chosen for this story], and she was very pretty. Some people called her beautiful. She had green eyes, dark brown hair, a sparkling smile, and a good figure. She had a way of kidding that attracted men. Other men thought I was very lucky to be married to her. After I left, I found out a whole lot of them called her up, hoping to get a date."

"Was she short or tall?"

"She was tall, even taller than your dad."

"You're not that tall, Daddy."

"Her feet were bigger than mine, too. But to answer your question, living with one wife cannot affect the looks of the children that may be made with another wife. In your case, you and your brothers are very fortunate because Mom is so pretty." I waited in vain for her to compliment my own looks.

While she mulled over my answer, it occurred to me suddenly that there was more to her question than she may have realized. Her question had reminded me of a remarkable, though almost forgotten episode in my earlier marriage. I began to tell Sara—and she was the first person ever to hear this story—about Cynthia's increasingly desperate efforts to become a mother. I told her about standing on the cobblestone sidewalk outside Central Park after Cynthia and I had visited a specialist on Fifth Avenue. She was hitting me on the chest with the sides of both of her fists, as women do in the movies when they're upset, because the doctor had said the possibility of pregnancy was remote and possibly dangerous. "'Damn you, damn you, damn you!' she kept saying."

(There followed over the next few months a series of increasingly strange and not particularly affectionate meetings in bed. I don't know where Cynthia had picked up these ideas and positions—from doctors, friends, library books, people on the street, hippie musicians, fortune tellers—but at times I felt more like a gymnast or a tumbler than a husband or a lover. None of this was conveyed to Sara.)

"We tried all kinds of different ways to start a baby. Do you know how husbands and wives start babies?" I asked her.

"Yes," she said, "Mom has told me all about it."

"Do you mind talking about it?" I asked.

"No, I don't but not so close to supper," she said. What a great daughter, I thought, she has my sense of humor.

"Had we been happy," I continued, "all these efforts might have given us some laughs. But as it turned out, all it did was make us feel more sad and distant from each other."

"Maybe," Sara said, "the problem was you and not Cynthia. Did you go to a Fifth Avenue specialist, too?"

There she had me. I had gotten a clean bill of health in a checkup but never pursued the possibility that I was the problem with conception. I told Sara that, and she frowned.

"Let me go on. One day Cynthia came to me with an idea. 'Go to the Middle East, go to Syria or Lebanon and meet a nice woman and have a baby with her and bring the baby to me.' She was serious. She insisted I think it over. She felt the plan was practical, knowing my affection for the Middle East, and that we could reunite in a year with the new baby."

I told Sara I had realized instantly that the notion, despite its fairy tale appeal, was unworkable, so I feigned contemplation over a period of several days. Eventually I had to tell Cynthia my decision. "'I'm afraid to carry out the idea,' I said. 'I'm afraid I would fall in love with the mother and want to stay with her and our baby. You would have no husband to hit on the chest, and no baby to love. I won't do it.'"

A surprising amount of time passed since Sara and I had first sat down. The sun brushed across the tops of the trees. A new breeze nudged us with the approaching dusk. The woods around us began to drape themselves in mystery. I had never until a moment ago made the connection between Cynthia's desire for a little Arab and the one who sat across from me. But it now seemed like a succession of events, part of an unusual but predictable order. It seemed important at that moment to ask Sara, "Would you like to meet Cynthia?"

I pictured telephoning her in the city. We'd not met since that last time in the lawyer's office. She would say yes and be charming and affectionate with my daughter and give her gifts. She would kid around. She would turn to me and say I'm looking older. A man would arrive and she would introduce her husband. We would leave, and she would cry and feel the pain of an ancient hurt.

Sara rose and came toward me. I stood and we hugged. My fingertips pressed into her ribs. I bent to kiss her and tasted the strap of her overalls. After a while we separated. "I'll race you back to the house," she said. "I think Mom's home."

Fishing

I held my ground, frightened but fascinated, as a bluefish threatened to pull my boy overboard and into the Plum Gut. "You got a smacker on there!" yelled Danny Kane. "Hold on, Charles!"

Charles set his feet and tucked in his elbows and hauled with all his might. The bluefish fought back so hard that Charles's heels flew off the deck, his chest slamming into the gunnel. The rip tide tossed us about. Under a bright, hazy sky, the Long Island water was an endless field of treasure, ten million untouchable diamonds. Danny started the engine to regain control of his boat. Charles hauled again, straining the rod. The bluefish lunged and raced toward the sea. When it looked as if Charles might follow the rod and the fish over the side, Danny nodded for me to take the wheel.

"You've almost got him, Old Man," he said to my son, who is eleven. "Let me give you a hand."

Charles carefully relinquished the rod, concerned that this shift in tactics might give the quarry some advantage. Danny skillfully played the fish, let him run, brought him back, let him run again, draining his energy and resolve. "I think you've got him now, Charles," said Danny, handling back the rod. "Bring him in carefully and slowly. That's it. No yanking. Nice and smooth."

Charles reeled laboriously, looking as though he were operating a crane instead of a boat rod. Lacking a net or gaff, Danny reached almost into the water and pulled the large fish, momentarily still, into the boat. The moment its body touched metal, the bluefish sprang in a fury. It danced wildly. It sprayed its blood in several directions, spattering the ice chest. With its long, dark and silver body, it punished the boat. "That's why they call it a smacker," said Danny, with satisfaction. "What a beauty." He slugged it on the head with the handle of a large scaling knife.

"What's its weight?" asked Charles.

"A good eight, nine pounds," said Danny.

"Twelve. Maybe fifteen," I said. "I jigged for blues for years, caught plenty, but never one this big." There was no protest from Danny Kane.

I felt as spent as Charles must have. While he had fought the fish, I had fought the reflex to protect him from the loss of the biggest fish he had ever hooked and a dunking—maybe worse—in the sea. I had anticipated this moment for several years, a moment that ten years from today might be forgotten but thirty years from now might be relished as important as his first kiss. I felt certain of it. But I had to wait to see whether Charles would remember this morning with joy or with fear. I looked his way and smiled tentatively. He looked toward me and down at the fish still fighting for life and turned to look out at the water.

Was it a memory, a dream, a story whispered behind closed doors at night? Maybe all of these. When I was small, Samuel, the boy across the street, and I went down to the harbor at Salem, Massachusetts, pushed a dory into the water, jumped in, and began our voyage, heading for the wintry Atlantic on the outgoing tide. I held Samuel responsible for forgetting the oars, although at age four we were hardly able to carry them and certainly unable to row with them. Dwelling in one of the cradles of democracy, Samuel and I decided to share the blame. We later told neighborhood chums impressed by our adventure that we each forgot one oar.

A boatyard worker working atop a peeling hull taller than a house spotted us and scampered down his wooden ladder and into a launch. The day was gray and cool, the water choppy. When he intercepted us and knotted a tow line, I could still see the roof of the house we lived in above the shoreline. I didn't resist the rescue. Returning home soaking wet, I was lectured, hectored, hugged, wrapped in blankets in my father's easy chair, and filled with hot chocolate. My older sister said I was stupid and almost drowned. Samuel's father was a rabbi, a gentle man, his face a study in forbearance with permanent dark rings under the eyes. He had been sent by a humorous God to this Judean frontier, where most of his neighbors were hostile French-Canadian Catholics. Samuel said that as a result of our dalliance, he was told to accelerate his Hebrew prayer studies. The event may have given my friend the religion of his father, but over time it gave me something entirely different. My beliefs became connected to the sea.

Charles, Danny, and I fished for another hour, moving often. I felt buoyed by the capture of the first blue. But there were no more. Other fishermen glided by, spreading their arms, hands palms up and shrugging, the universal language of the disappointed seeker of the fish. But we had our prize, now calm and probably dead among the colas and beers in the splattered freezer. No one argued when Danny suggested we head back to Orient Point. The hazy sunlight had slyly burnt us, but we wouldn't feel it until we were indoors.

"Take the wheel, Old Man," Danny Kane ordered. Charles leapt up, grasped the centerboard controls, gave the throttle a tap, and squinted through the Plexiglas windshield, then to starboard and port. I sat in the stern of the twenty-five-footer as Danny bustled about. I wanted to catch Charles's attention and let him know I was admiring him, but an instinct as deep as the water below us told me to look away. To smile at him now would be to reduce him to a little boy, and at this moment he was not a little boy. The alert boat builder in Salem Harbor had done the right thing for me; today, I would do as much for Charles.

Sara and Edward, Charles's sister and brother, were bold as little children, racing into the water the moment we arrived at our rented house on the bay at Cutchogue, Long Island. They were even bolder challenging the waves of the Sound. Only the crashing surf at Amagansett gave them pause, and then on days when only fools and daredevils ventured in. But Charles hung back, tentative and cautious. At age four, I blithely set out to sea in a dory. At age four, Charles did not touch the water of Long Island Sound until I invented a game to coax him.

He would climb on my shoulders, and I marched up and down the sand and then, after a while, turned toward the water. "Let's take a step," I would sing. "And another step, and another step," all the time immersing myself in the gentle surf, hunching down like Groucho Marx without a cigar, hoping to immerse Charles. The first several times he protested he was getting wet over his knees, while I almost suffocated beneath him. But he finally got wet all over and spent the rest of the day racing into the water, returning to our blanket to announce he'd raced into the water and then racing back in again. When I tried to put him back on my shoulders, he dismissed the ploy as a game for infants. He celebrated his baptism by polishing off a bag of dried fruit. "I love africots," I remember him saying. The beautiful lifeguard, brown and powerful behind mirrored glassed, watched us, as she had for several days. Charles and I approached her so I could flirt. "I saw you today," she said to my boy. "Good job." She filled him with pleasure and ignored me. When we arrived back at our blanket, Charles's mother said, "Charles, first you dip in the water like a champion, then you flirt with the lifeguard. What a guy." She knew all, and she had already forgiven me.

"A little more speed," said Danny, and Charles nodded seriously and tapped the throttle again. I looked at my son and my friend and felt love for both of them. At Orient Point, we maneuvered the boat back onto its trailer, pulled into a lot paved with broken shells and headed for a restaurant called Orient by the Sea. Outside on the deck, a young woman in high-cut white shorts and a halter sipped a tall drink and chatted with two people who appeared to be her parents. Danny and I exchanged glances. Charles walked ahead and into the bar. We had set out from the Motel on the Bay in South Jamesport at five o'clock, nine hours ago, and we were thirsty.

"Any luck, boys?" asked the pretty bartender.

"Charles here pulled in the smacker to end all smackers," said Danny. I began to hug Charles around the shoulders, but he shrugged me off. "How about rum and coke?" Danny asked. We all nodded. The bartender poured identical-looking drinks, inconspicuously omitting the rum from Charles's. Charles stepped up to the bar and wrapped his hand around the cold glass on its coaster. In the dim light of the bar, the dark woods swallowing reflections, the sun blazing outside the windows, our burned faces starting to smart, I saw him swagger as he reached for the drink made by the woman who had just learned he had caught a huge blue.

The ride on Route 25 back to the motel, where wives and mothers and children waited, seemed endless now. It had been exciting and brief at daybreak. Danny drove the pickup, the boat and the trailer making comforting rattling noises behind us. In the middle of the high, ramshackle cab Charles was silent and stared at the road.

A few minutes later, his head brushed my shoulder and did not move for a half-hour. His hair was summer blond and smelled of salt. He breathed through his mouth. In sleep, he was a boy again.

Roles

I stared shamelessly into her blue eyes. Still lovely, they were tired and moist as eyes are when they have been open most of the night. "When can I see you again?" I asked. She smiled and paused to think. "Tonight. Six o'clock. I'll be hungry but don't fuss." That's how it's been since my wife and I—and our three children—began our new way of life.

She is a full-time law student, studying long and hard, and we are very proud of her. I still call her "dear" and "sweetie pie" but I can tell she especially loves it when I say, "Counselor, is fettuccini all right tonight?"

I gave up a nine-to-five life in the city. My routine now includes writing newspaper and magazine pieces, putting together stories for a book and tolerating it when men I run into grin and say, "I never met a Mr. Mom in real life before." That doesn't bother me. Imagined or not, I think I hear envy in their voices. Most of them drive or commute long distances, using up endless hours of time and energy that I can apply to paper (as in writing) or to pasta (as in most of my dinner menus).

It sounds too noble to say I came home so Evelyn could pursue her dream. The children are already eleven, ten, and eight. The school bus drops them off right in our driveway. They are capable of making their own peanut butter sandwiches (though amazingly unskilled in cleaning up the ensuing mess) and can tolerate a few hours each day as latchkey urchins. I did it because working at home and helping out was my dream, too.

Most men spend their lifetime avoiding domestic chores. They brag that they hate shopping. But I find an hour or so in a giant supermarket gathering food for my family an adventure. Where else could you indulge in impulses, pay for them, and go home and eat them? I do windows. I happen to enjoy the sparkle that appears when you've run paper towels over window cleaner. My technique is to blame the children for every mess. I've already threatened to banish them from so many rooms of our modest home that if I carried out these threats, they'd be living in the neighbor's tree house.

Starting in my bachelor days, I became a believer in the tidy-and-beyond-that-who-cares approach to home care. The counselor objects. If anything, she believes a home should be clean if casual. She does not understand why month-old daily newspapers must remain in the living and dining rooms, no matter how neatly stacked, if the children are excluded. Life becomes a compromise. The children and the newspapers share the rooms. The look achieved is Early Earthquake.

We have a dishwasher, but I happen to find sensual pleasure in washing dishes. I don't think that's so weird. Think of the warmth of water flowing over the hands (I refuse to use rubber gloves), the bouquet of the detergent rising to the nostrils, and the satisfaction to the eye, after vigorous scrubbing, of the gleaming pot. Then there's the downside of dealing with what was in the pot. I get the creeps scooping up the soggy scraps of noodles, like so many dead yellow worms, from the bottom of the sink.

"There's another sensual experience waiting for you downstairs," Evelyn has started to point out. For reasons not yet fully understood, I avoid using the washing machine. I don't know how to use it. My children know how to use it. I don't mind washing items by hand. I don't mind hanging clothes outdoors. I don't mind (occasionally) ironing. My only explanation is that I have always avoided machines as long as I could. I waited ten years before buying a computer, hoping all the while computers would just go away and leave me alone.

There's another important sensual subject, sensuality itself. I have to admit that when Evelyn began school, I feared a three-year recess in our romantic life. True, back rubs these evenings often lead to … more back rubs, but my fears were groundless. Her studies in fact have sparked in an already vivacious woman a brand-new source of vitality.

My experience over the last months did not prepare me, however, for the meeting with the Little League coach. I'd taken the children to a post-season picnic; the chauffeur's cap is another one of the hats I wear these days. I spotted the burly, likeable coach. He had a small package tucked under his arm. We shook hands, and when he asked about my wife, I informed him of her admission to law school and the determined way she had hit the books.

"Gonna be a gigolo, huh?" he said.

I flustered over my reply, explaining that I was working hard at the writing as well as taking care of many of the household chores. He wasn't buying my explanation.

"My wife wanted to go to work too," he told me. "I said no and she fought me on it and took a part-time job anyway. She's teaching. And now that her birthday's coming up, I got her the perfect gift."

He pulled a box out of the bag he was carrying and showed it to me with satisfaction. It contained a pair of suspenders. I smiled but was embarrassed. Deep down, I felt sorry for him. On the way home I pondered what to get for Evelyn's birthday, which was coming up. The children helped me decide. We presented her with a briefcase, the wide, deep kind law students and lawyers need for their books and papers. Her reaction was wonderful, but I can't tell you any more than that. The counselor has informed me that that is privileged information.

Joe and Me

When I was a boy, we whispered about other people's fathers. They came home after dark in a fury. Through closed windows and drawn shades flew anger and insanity. Pots crashed. Furniture shattered. Children cried. I heard a woman say, "No, Joe, no!" Sometimes the man threw open the windows. "Did you hear enough?" he shouted. The family lived in shame then or moved.

I was afraid of meeting these men in the daytime on the street. I was afraid of looking at them. I was afraid they would grab me by the neck and throw me into a fence or a hedge. But they only walked by, carrying their evening newspaper rolled under an arm. Their faces looked tired and gentle. Sometimes they stopped and asked about my mother and father. I said, "fine, thank you" and turned crimson due to the feelings I was trying to conceal

Every now and then, one of these men went to the corner for a pack of Camels or a loaf of bread and didn't come back. Only later did I learn that the trip to the store was a metaphor. I couldn't decide if that walk was a flight by the man or a sentence handed down by his wife, family, and neighbors. I still don't know. But the man lived afterward only in rumors.

Someone visiting New York City claimed to have seen him boarding a subway train in Times Square. "Joe!" he shouted. Joe didn't hear or didn't want to answer. He was still wearing his brown felt hat and leather jacket. How did he get there? I wondered. Who was he with? Was it a woman? Was she beautiful? No one had the answers. Another time we heard he'd been spotted at night taking tickets and operating the merry-go-round in Old Orchard Beach, Maine.

Last week, I felt a storm coming on for two or three days. I tried to turn my back on it, as I had a few times before, but it seemed to swirl all around me. By Saturday, I was hollering at my sons for directing me to the wrong field for Little League practice. I had forgotten I'd said it was no problem, that we'd swing by both fields. "Dad," said Edward, who is approaching twelve, "I don't understand you anymore." On the way home, I bought them ice cream cones.

At the house, I railed against a classmate of Charles, an eleven-year-old who thinks he can disguise his sly disrespect behind good manners. On a visit a few days earlier, he'd opened the door to my home office upstairs and said, "Hello, Mr. Hadad," while I worked at the computer and conducted an interview on the telephone.

"I've got his number and he's a jerk and you're a jerk if you don't see it," I said. Charles became upset, his face turned dark. He shouted, "He is not!" and was ready to cry. The exchange attracted my wife Evelyn, who defended Charles and his friend. "This community is so small, who else would you ask over?" she said. "Why don't you give us a list of who is acceptable?" She continued preparing supper.

I waited impatiently until the day was only a shadow and made a martini. It felt good and warm. As a lightness rose in my head, I pictured a great flurry of activity in the brain, an immense miniature railroad system, with the tracks and trains and switches and schedules all being rearranged on order of the alcohol. Reaching for my wallet, I sought out my third child, Sara, who is eight years old. She was playing with the plush zoo she keeps in her bedroom. I knocked and went in. "Here's your allowance," I said. She took it, thanked me, counted it, and looked up, shyly. "You're one short," she said. I had given her four singles and hidden another in my waistband. It was part of my training on developing respect for money. But her wariness annoyed me. I wanted her to be her sassy self, I wanted her to say, "Nice try, Daddy, but you know better than I do, the official figure is five big ones." I handed over the fifth bill and returned to the kitchen.

I poured a second gin and added a few ice cubes. I'd forgotten about the olive, still at the bottom of the tumbler. I skipped the vermouth. I read a lengthy article about the Mafia but felt I had learned nothing new when it was over. I had heard the Mafia likes to read about itself. Would the criminals threaten the author or send him flowers and a thank-you note? I read a column about the relationship between parsimony and paranoia, and I thought I'd send it to my in-laws. I pictured them waving the article in extreme agitation and pacing around their kitchen cursing me. That pleased me, and I enjoyed a sardonic laugh. I suddenly decided I was starving. "Where's dinner?" I demanded of the empty living room.

In several minutes, the table had been set. Bread and salad had been put out. At each place, there was a steaming dish of lasagna. Evelyn had spent an afternoon making it. I sat and stared at it and decided I hated lasagna. The children began to eat. I picked up my plate and balanced it in my palm and aimed it at her. "Here's what I think of the food and the service and the kindness that exists in this poor excuse for a home!" I said. No one lived close enough to hear. I didn't care if they did.

The children gasped. "No, Dad, no," said the smallest. My wife stood her ground, asked for no explanation, stared me in the eye, waited for the splatter. I put the plate down and left the dining room.

The downstairs soon emptied. I swaggered around, enjoying the solitude. I went to the cellar for one of the two or three good red wines we possessed, opened it, found the good crystal. I plunked both down on the limestone hearth, making all the noise I could, and began to drink. It was beautiful wine, lush and dry, and for a moment I wanted to pour a glass for Evelyn, but that was out of the question.

I put Benny Goodman music on. Tonight there would be no infernal television or video games. I felt the insinuating rhythms and seductive clarinet, almost on my skin. "Memories of You" and "Body and Soul" and "Don't Be That Way" came out of the speaker. That's what I figured they were saying upstairs. Don't be that way. These were the same kinds of tunes that floated through the windows in the old neighborhood on warm nights when there was no trouble. I hadn't slugged anyone or broken anything. But I was the tyrant just the same. I understood now about those men so long ago.

An hour later, my daughter appeared in the living room. She hugged me around the waist, like a child getting its arms around a tree. I cradled her head against my ribs. My instinct might have been to say something to soothe her and explain away her confusion, but I had nothing to say. I felt mean as I released her and went to bed.

The next morning, with very little communication, we all drove to a running track. Evelyn and I were supposed to jog while the children played on the infield. I ran a few laps by myself, too slow for my wife, and spied the children. They had made up a game. They were climbing a chain-link batting cage and using it as a diving platform to leap onto a pile of exercise cushions. It looked dangerous but exhilarating.

I did not try to approach them. Did they think I might pick them up and hurl them against a fence? I only wanted to ask how they were, how their mother was. I felt I was watching an old home movie of my family in happier times. After a while Sara slipped away and joined me on the track. We had not spoken since the exchange over the allowance. She wore her blue Yankees jacket. Her feet were wet from the soggy grass, and the scar near her knee from a fall two summers ago was still visible. We walked as her mother ran smoothly in the distance.

"Sometimes a person has to blow his stack," I said after a while to break the silence. "I don't know exactly why. It could be an insult by a store clerk or a rude motorist. It could be finding out a friend is untrue, or an unpaid bill, an unsold story. It could be all of those things added up."

She looked up to show she was paying attention. Hair fell over one of the brown eyes.

"Some men snap in an office or at a party or in a barroom. I did it last night at home."

We kept moving. Her silence was unnerving.

"Take me back," I said.

"Can I go see Edward and Charles?" she replied.

In a few minutes the three children were taking turns again, climbing the cage, leaping, bouncing, and starting all over. In between, I knew they were talking it over, weighing how I had treated their mother, holding court, passing judgment. I started to run again. I felt it was essential to stay in motion while they decided, convinced that the longer they took and the more tired I became, the better were my chances. I was finally exhausted. My legs throbbed. I felt sick to my stomach. I stopped and waved. They picked up their jackets and started over. Was Sara smiling? I think she was smiling.

Almost True

I am an ordinary man. This is not a matter of pride or a comfort because I, like everyone else, would like to feel special in some way. But whether going to the mailbox, hiking in the woods, stopping by the market, boarding the commuter train, I am just another face and body, neither more nor less interesting than the next.

I like my family. They, if anything, make me feel special. I carry photographs in my wallet, updating some of them every year, keeping favorites indefinitely, although I can't remember the last time anyone asked to look at them. I look at them. Slipping out the plastic identity card that allows me to pay with a check at the supermarket, I tend to pause and look at the photograph of my three children, shoulder to shoulder, grinning and clowning for the camera, only half as tall as the sunflowers behind them. The picture makes me smile.

I carry photographs in my wallet and tableaux in my mind. I sometimes become infatuated with tableaux, like the one in the picture with the sunflowers, or the three of them frolicking in the sand and sea grass by the ocean, or even curled up on the sofa, like a pack of exhausted puppies, listening to their mother read.

I flip the plastic sleeves to a photograph of my wife finishing a road race in Central Park, her arm and shoulder muscles taut with weariness and determination, her pony tail slapping the back of her head. Her face is so open and earnest as well as so pretty. A woman behind me loudly clears her throat. "Do you want to see the pictures?" I ask. She is annoyed at my sarcasm, and I suppose I am annoyed at being interrupted in my reverie, but I hastily hand the identity card and check over to the cashier.

I wonder if other fathers experience a very different kind of tableau: On a warm and fragrant afternoon, several hours before dusk, I pull into the driveway after a day in the city. I look for the children, skateboarding or tossing a baseball back and forth. Maybe Evelyn is home from her studies and outside with them, playing with our dog Rex. I look for a scene that I have imagined, off and on, all the way home. No one is visible. The house is silent.

This is what I imagine next: A man, usually only one man, leaves the nearby highway, drives up our road and decided to pull in at our house. He is slim and dressed in casual clothes. Sometimes he is white, sometimes he is black. It is a Friday. The man enters the house, and a short time later leaves. I enter, Charles, who fights perpetually with Sara, has his arm draped across her shoulder. Edward lies next to Evelyn.

A few seconds later, Edward glides out of the garage on his skateboard. I slump on the driver's seat. "Hi, Dad," he says, holding a plastic glass of lemonade, offering a sip. "Train late?"

"No, dear," I say, "I had some extra work to clean up. I took a later train. Where are Charles and Sara and your mother?"

"Charles is playing over at Justin's house. Mom and Sara went shopping."

I step out of the car and hug him. He hugs me back. When we separate, he has a quizzical look on his face. "What's the matter, I'm not allowed to love my elder son?" I say. It doesn't clear the air. He knows that adults, like children, lead double lives. He speeds off on his board.

At other times, the imagined scenes are not so paralyzing, only frightening. I hear a scream and expect to find broken limbs and punctured skin. I race up the steps to find the children laughing at a movie on television. Often their complaints are couched in shouts and tears. "You'll kill me yet by crying wolf one time too often," I say. My relief overcomes my annoyance.

"Dear Family," I write. I have been working at home this day and arrive at a decision. It feels absolutely right. Once decided, I have trouble even imagining any alternative. "I have to go to the city to take care of a friend. Please don't worry." It's not extraordinary that I would respond to a call for help. It's a value I try to instill in the children. I know they'll begin to worry anyhow, the moment they see the note. There's nothing I can do about that. "I'll try to call later. Love, Dad."

I dress in business clothes and drive to the station. On the train ride to the city I read a newspaper clipping about a boy several times. The story says he was kidnapped by a neighborhood bully and taken to the basement of a building, where he was tied with rags to a pipe. The bully tried to abuse him in many ways. The boy resisted and was beaten. The bully then poured kerosene over him and lit a match. The flames burned the rags, and the boy pulled free and ran into the street, where some men knocked him to the ground and rolled him over until the flames were out. The story is accompanied by a photograph apparently taken by an untalented and indifferent school photographer. The boy looks unhappy and is staring listlessly into the lens.

At Grand Central, I take the Lexington Avenue subway uptown and arrive at the entrance to the hospital. It is built in a series of towers, an edifice to the glory of medicine, a cathedral where the infirm enter hopeful and unquestioning. I imagine many young doctors have been moved to tears when they first enter its portals.

"Maurice LaFleur," I say to the attractive but arch-looking woman at the information desk in the lobby. She is not going to tell me where to find him. I lower my voice. "I'm the family attorney," I say. "Room 1505; take the elevator to your left," she says. Regular people can't scare medical people, but lawyers can.

The floor is quiet, and outside Room 1505, a large man in an open shirt and windbreaker sits in a chair with his head in his hands. He ignores me, and I peek into the room. A small figure in the bed appears to be asleep. All that is visible is a forehead, a place for a parent's lips.

"Excuse me," I say to the man. He raises his head. His face is tense and strained. In his eyes, he looks insane. "I want to make a donation," I tell him.

He exhales heavily and tries to be polite. "T'ank you, man. Dey start some kind of fund for my boy. Go and see de nurse down de hall. She give you the address." He puts his head back in his hands.

"I don't want to give money," I say. He looks up. He is angry that I'm still there.

"What you want to give?" he says. It sounds like a growl.

"I want to make a donation. Part of me."

He jumps out of the chair. "Get out of here. Get away from me."

"Maurice is going to need new skin. I am here to give him some of mine."

"My Maurice is a black boy, you are white. You are crazy, man."

~212~

"What's the difference? I'm healthy. We've got to make him healthy again. Who's going to care if Maurice has a white patch here and there? You worried bigots will laugh at Maurice on the beach?"

Mr. LaFleur stares into my eyes, looks around as if I am part of some elaborate, horrible joke. No one else is on the dimly lit floor.

"I am prepared to be admitted right now. Arm, thigh, hip, back, stomach. Whatever the doctors need for Maurice I am willing to give. I'm a father, just like you."

Mr. LaFleur raises his arm and his hand comes toward me. I have trouble telling whether he's going to throw a punch. I flinch but stand my ground. He grabs my hand and shakes it. "T'ank you," he says, and he falls back into his chair.

At the nurses' station I explain my presence, and the agreement just negotiated with Mr. LaFleur. Two nurses look at each other. "Are you serious?" says one of them. The question sounds cruel. "I'm perfectly sane," I tell them. "It's something I want to do for Maurice."

"People don't donate skin," says the nurse who appears to be in charge. "Sometimes parents or relatives do, but I can assure you it is an excruciatingly painful procedure." Her words frighten me. "I can take it," I say.

"We prefer to use the skin of a cadaver," she goes on in a monotone. "In either case, donated skin or cadaver skin, the recipient rejects it after six or eight weeks. All it does is buy time. Ultimately we will use Maurice's own skin and, if necessary, take culture tissue from his body and grow new skin." They wait like lecturers for any last questions from the back of the room. They don't say thank you or good-bye.

On the train ride home I fall asleep, awakened only by the conductor's hand jiggling my shoulder. I've missed my stop, and we're at the end of the line. I telephone Evelyn from the deserted station and ask her to pick me up. As we pull out of the station, I look out at the Hudson River, to the cliff that always reminds me of a bison's head and shoulders. It's there, pushing against the river. We pick up speed as the car darts toward home on the two-lane highway. As we pass the French restaurant I tell Evelyn to be careful, to slow down on the downhill curve. She becomes annoyed, as she always does, at my instruction but slows down, as she always does.

I tell her where I've been. She listens silently and a long time passes. We pull off the highway and onto the road that leads to our house. She finally speaks. "Why?" she says.

"Because it didn't happen to ours," I tell her.

Going on Twelve

A trying-on of beliefs is occurring between Edward and me, the effort at a new order, the striking of a different balance. It is not an easy time. He will be twelve years old next week. As they used to say in my old seaside neighborhood of Salem, Massachusetts, Edward's approaching Peabody.

He keeps in his bedroom a postcard of nearly naked women strolling on the beach at Rio de Janeiro. We walk in the woods, and I encourage him to ask anything he wants about the facts of life, privately hoping I can handle the questions. One afternoon he announces there is something he'd like to know.

"Shoot, pal," I say, pleased at his trust. He asks about the difference between various kinds of sanitary napkins. I answer, laughing inside with a curious kind of joy.

Sometimes on walks we find condoms along the roadside. They excite his curiosity, but all he says is, "They look like squashed slugs." I try to demystify the subject by telling him the universal story: getting up the nerve to ask the druggist to open that little wooden drawer behind the counter and sell me a three-pack, carrying them in my wallet—the sexual Boy Scout ever prepared—until they were old and dry and good only for laughs and good-natured ridicule from my fellow sexual Scouts.

Newspaper and magazine stories about children with active sex lives scare and confuse me. I tell Edward that he'd better come to me before he ever tries anything fancy, or I'll be very upset. I think he enjoys the invitation and the threat, but he only smiles.

I drive him and his male and female classmates to the movie theater on the highway, and he cautions me not to say anything to embarrass him. I peer at the girls through the rearview mirror and decide they are too innocent and young for anything but a smooch, if that, but

I really don't know. As we pull up, I read the movie billboard. "PG-13," I say. "Have you all been given parental guidance?" They find the question humorous. I suspect they whisper that Edward's father is a total square.

I ask him what he would like for his birthday, and he works up a list. I find it endearing—baseball cards, a mitt, a Walkman, and audio tapes, a Nintendo game, money. "I'll do the best I can but it'll be only one or two of these things," I tell him. Next to the money I write, "$1 million." It says what I would want to do for him. He beams, and it's as good as a long hug.

Around the house, Edward is kind and helpful one moment, moody and furtive the next. Some mornings he races out the door without a good-bye; on others, he pauses and kisses me on the lips. As I savor that kiss, I wonder about the depth of my ability to guide him into adolescence. I wonder why I holler at him or why, the other day, I became so enraged when his noisiness woke his mother from a nap that I tossed the bentwood rocker. A moment later I felt like the old bear who seizes the cub's neck with his teeth, never to bite, only to warn. He finds it painful to apologize but comes up behind me and says very quietly, "I'm sorry, Dad."

But on a recent night, I awake at three o'clock in the morning in a state of despair, convinced I have lost him, that there will be, until he grows up and leaves home, nothing between us but formal ritual. In the morning I hold my breath as he enters the kitchen. Nothing seems different. The school bus arrives. "Bye, Dad," he says and puts up his face for a kiss. When the bus is down the driveway, I weep with relief.

He buys me a yellow cap with the words "World's Coolest Dad" on it. I wear it at a Little League game but feel very self-conscious. I realize I feel unworthy. I begin leaving the cap in the car trunk. He doesn't ask about it.

Edward says one day he hates his middle name—Salim, the name of his grandfather's eldest brother—but would keep it if his full name became Edward Salim Herbert Hadad. I didn't think anyone ever really wanted to be named Herbert. I am so astounded by his choice it is not until later that I feel touched.

His viewing habits are a source of perpetual worry. He, his brother Charles, and his buddies play gruesome video games like Contra, in which a solitary, bare-chested man with an automatic gun tries to survive in a world of relentless warfare. Weary of a day of slaughter in the jungle, they switch on cable television and sit in awe at what I consider soft-core pornography, a pseudo-documentary about the making of the *Sports Illustrated* annual swimsuit issue. On a visit to a business office, I find a roomful of men watching the same program. I can't decide if the men have childish taste or the children have grownup taste or if there isn't any substantial difference.

Beautiful young women at exotic seasides stand around or pose on cue in skimpy bathing suits while photographers and assistants race around, anointing them with a pitcher of water to make their skin glisten, or telling them how wonderful they appear to the eye of the camera. I don't order the boys to turn off the television set because that would make me a fraud. I want to see the bodies, too.

"When were you on the cover?" an older woman in a safari outfit asks a preening, nearly nude beauty as I enter the room.

"Eighty-six," the woman answers.

"Nineteen eighty-six?" asks the director.

"No, 1886," I say.

Edward, Charles, and a friend named Matt on a sleepover visit laugh loudly, the only laugh they'll get out of the show and a welcome release from the near boiling point to which all those hormones have been raised. Frankly, I'm impressed that the cover girl is still out there, years after her triumph, preening with the rest of them.

"You guys hungry?" I ask the gang.

"We'll get something in a little while," says Edward.

"We've got some nice fresh bread and cold cuts."

No answer.

"And don't forget the frozen Band-Aids."

Silence, except for the squealing bathing beauties dipping in the water and some man looking at the sky and predicting a squall. Will they finish their photo shoot, or will the skies open and the wind rise and just ruin everything? What drama!

"Anyone hear me? Don't you want to know what the frozen Band-Aids are for?"

"Cold cuts," says Edward blandly, never taking his eyes off the screen.

So what if I've told that joke a few times before, I say to myself. How many parents go out of their way to be entertaining? I would have laughed if my father had told the joke. I would have said, "I remember that from a long time ago, Dad, but it's still funny."

I later say something my dad wouldn't have dreamed of saying to me. Edward and Matt have made and received scores of telephone calls to and from the girls in their class, discussing one of their weekend visits to the movies as if they were planning the landing at Normandy. As they pause between calls, I happen by the kitchen phone to pick up my shoes left by the door to dry after a storm.

"Since you guys are stepping out tonight you may need these," I say, holding up and dangling a pair of rubbers. They look at each other and back at me and burst into nervous laughter. I laugh, too. But I feel too late I've tricked them into appreciating my joke. The subject's too shocking. I take refuge from my own bad taste by becoming testy and telling them I'm getting tired of being a taxi service. I know the role of chauffeur has only just begun. But fathers are allowed to be moody, too.

The weekend includes a birthday party invitation. I am pleased to learn the birthday girl is comfortable enough to have invited both girls and boys. I decide to offer Edward some etiquette guidelines. "After you offer the gift, you'll want to express your good wishes. First, slip your hand gently into the small of her back, and as she responds, ease forward and deliver the message. Since her name is Michelle, you may want to make it even more romantic, as in, 'Ah, Me-shell,' but that is optional. Then plant le Kiss gently on la Lips." Edward and the other boys are certain that I am stark mad.

Tonight a brief discussion leads to the decision to partake of nature's perfect food. I call and place our usual order: two large cheese pizzas, slightly undercooked, to take out. We like to reheat them in the oven, sometimes adding our own toppings. On the ride down I think back to a time before Edward was born. I was alone with the pizzeria owner waiting for my order when he decided to confide his philosophy.

"Make babies as long as you can," he said. "That way, you'll have a little bambino to sit in your lap when you're an old man." One day, when his children number seven, I ask him why the babies have stopped. He smiles but declines to answer. His wife nearby is quiet.

It is obvious she has finally thrown up her hands and said, "Basta!" I feel I know much about them. I like the family. I wish I knew how to pronounce the name.

"Oh, no, Dad. I know what you're going to do," Edward says. "You're going to go in and say, 'Excuse me, my son has a question. He wants to know if you like to be called Rizzo or Ritzo.' Dad, don't do it. It's embarrassing. Besides, I know the children. They all say 'Rizzo.'"

I make a little speech about people proud of their names who nonetheless alter them out of some idea of sounding more American. "For years I said our name was Hah-dad, like I was laughing at my own name. Instead of the subtle, proper Arabic, Heh-daad. I suspect that Signor and Signora Reet-zoh are doing the same sort of thing. But if it worries you, I'll keep it to myself."

In the modest restaurant, the husband is pounding and stretching the powdered dough for new pizzas; his wife is boxing the freshly made pies; and their eldest daughter, a girl of about fifteen, is wielding the long-handled paddle, examining the progress of the pizzas in the oven. I enjoy the scene. I take comfort from the familiar sight of a family working together. I admire it and assign to it profound meaning.

The mother looks up and reaches for our two pizzas, kept warm atop the ovens. "Ah, you know us," I say. "When I walk in the door you must say to yourself, 'Here comes Mr. Undercook.'" She smiles faintly. I feel Edward starting to shrink under the counter. Mrs. Rizzo is a lovely woman, slim and dark-haired and fair. To stroke her skin, I imagine, would be to feel a surface that somehow is both marble and mozzarella. She is invariably friendly but never flirtatious. Her daughter, who is already becoming beautiful, is so intent on the pizzas she ignores the people and the talk around her.

As our pizza boxes are tied with red twine, I look toward the girl and say to Mrs. Rizzo, "Who is that? Is that your sister visiting from Italy?"

A tomato-sauce color spreads across Mrs. Rizzo's face. A shimmer of pleasure ripples her apron.

"No, that's my daughter!" she says.

"Oh, I was mistaken. I'm sorry."

"That's all right. Don't apologize," says Mrs. Rizzo. I can all but taste her smile. Edward watches and listens and is fascinated.

On the ride home he's forgotten about the silly Mr. Undercook. Maybe, I can almost see him thinking, he's been a bit too hasty in his judgment. Maybe this old man can teach him a thing or two. We all dine on pizza and hope.

Afterword

When the three children were small, I began to count our wealth not by the size of a slim stock portfolio but by the number of years, God willing, we'd all be together before they were off to college or the workaday world. Evelyn, we're rich, I'd say, thirty-four more years, thirty-four golden years. But too soon it was ten years, five, one, and then none. They completed college and established exciting lives for themselves in Manhattan. Edward Salim, the self-conscious little boy in the pizzeria, won success in finance and then embarked on a sixteen-month odyssey around the world. Charles Aram, our shy child, parlayed a summer internship at the Cable News Network (CNN) into a full-time job and today is a talented and hard-driving producer and an occasional on-air correspondent. Sara Jameela spent two years in Prague teaching English to Czech executives while assembling a community of Czech and expatriate friends that persist to this day. Most recently, she completed a graduate degree in global affairs in preparation for a career in diplomacy and international policy.

Evelyn and I missed the children when they left, of course. We tensed for the jolt of the empty nest and made it different by having the house painted inside and out. But much to our delight, we also found that we still liked and loved each other. These days we relish a visit, a phone call, or an e-mail from the children. We meet them for dinner, a play, or a ball game. They come home every so often and we swap advice on careers and people. We reminisce about the times the parents and children grew up together, and the dramas, happy and sad, that played out within the walls of our home. We talk about giving up our sizeable house by the woods for a condo by the river or in a nearby town. Charles came by not so long ago and made a surprising remark. It made us rethink our plans, and his request became words we now cherish.

"I'll understand if you sell the house," he said, "but please don't let them tear it down. I want to come by one day with my wife and children and say to them, 'This is the house where I grew up.'" To me those words carried the whiff of immortality. Should we have concentrated on assembling an extensive portfolio for our future and theirs or immersed ourselves in the joyous details of raising a family? Every family is different, but for us it was the best decision we ever made.